EP/Volume 3

Post-craft

Sternberg Press

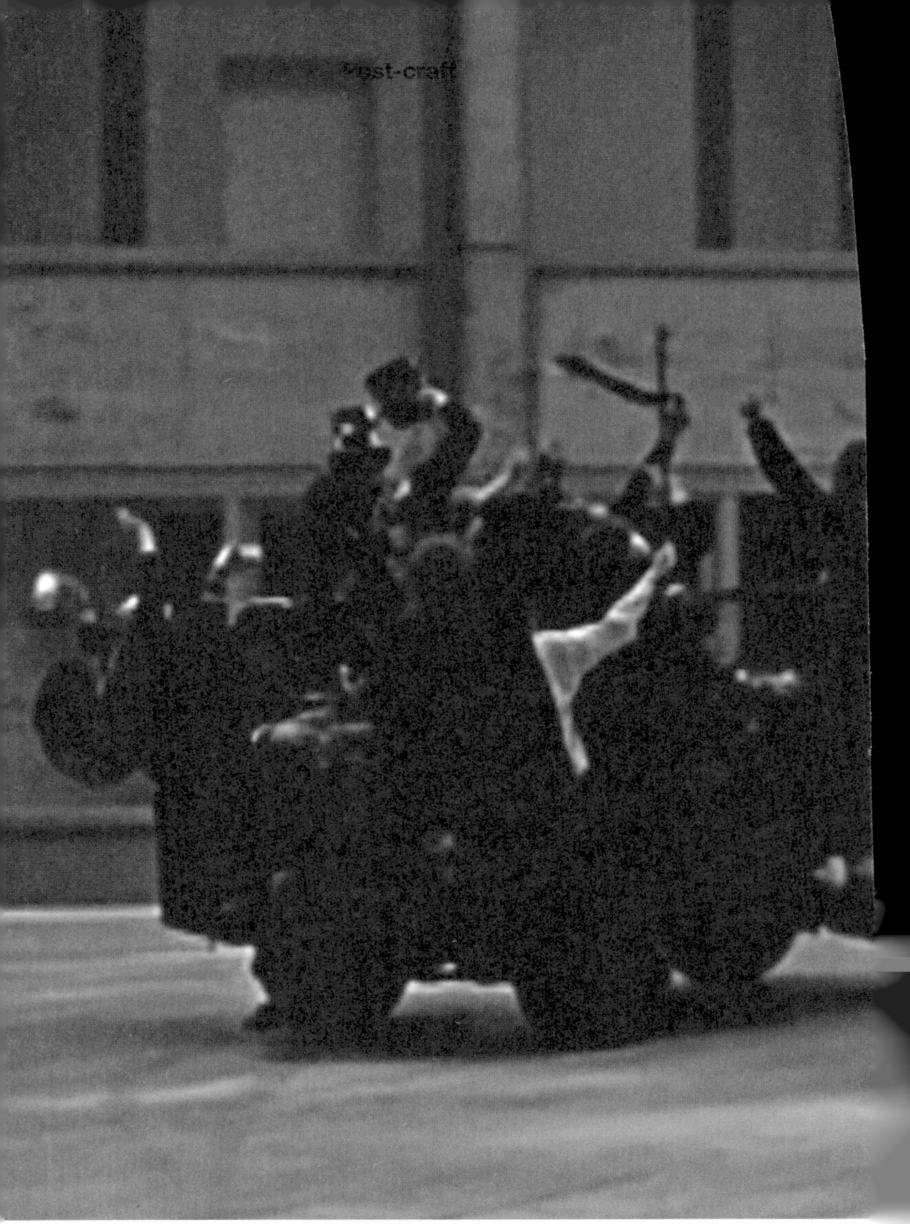

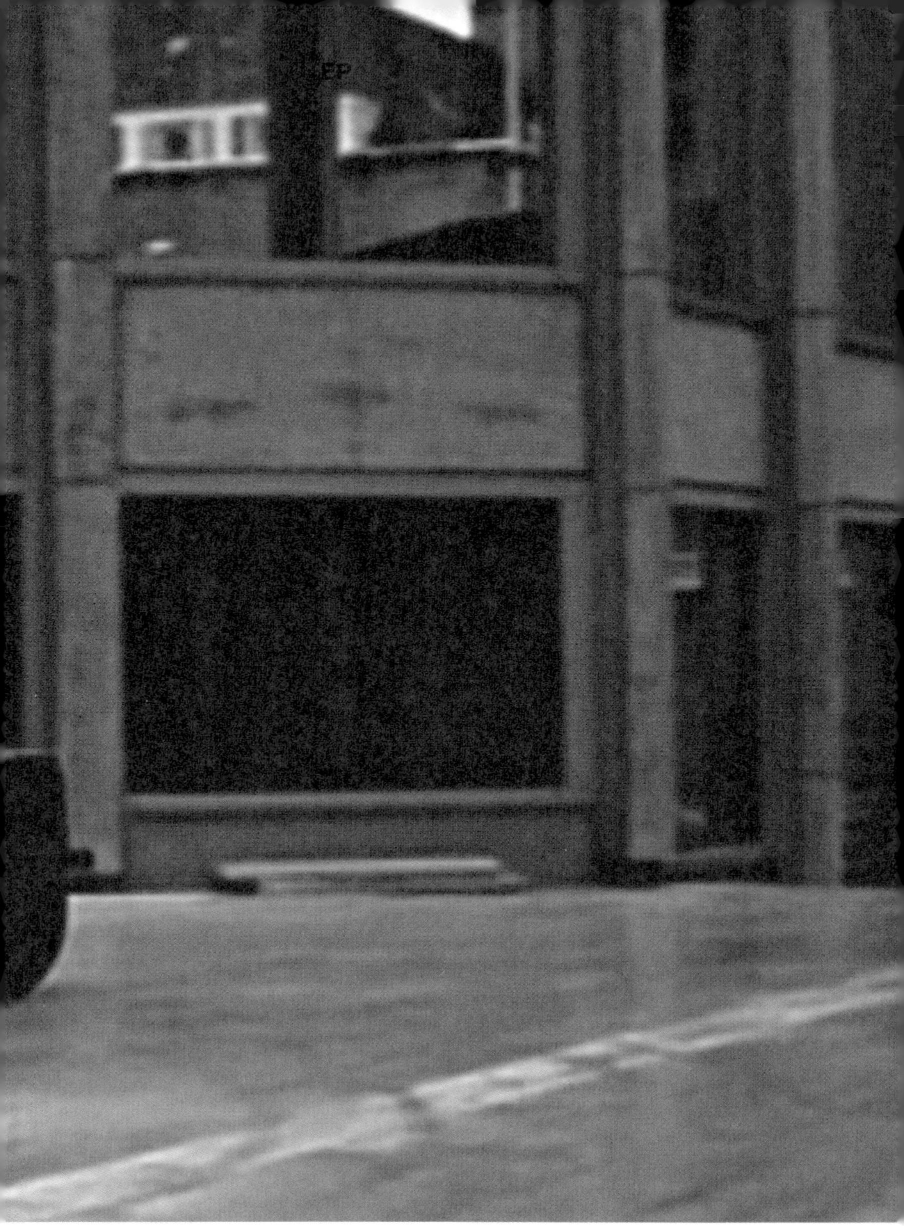

Post-craft

Pages 2–3:

The Economist Plaza (1959–64), London, by architects Alison and Peter Smithson, in the film *Blow-Up* (1966) by Michelangelo Antonioni.

Glenn Adamson is a curator and writer who works at the intersection of craft, design history, and contemporary art.

John Roberts is Professor of Art & Aesthetics in the Faculty of Arts and Social Sciences, University of Wolverhampton.

Clare Twomey is a London-based visual artist and researcher working in performance serial production, and site-specific installation.

Richard Sennett is the Centennial Professor of Sociology at the London School of Economics and University Professor of the Humanities at New York University.

Flore de Taisne and Edmund le Brun are founders of Ishkar, a retail platform for designers in countries such as Afghanistan, Yemen, and Pakistan.

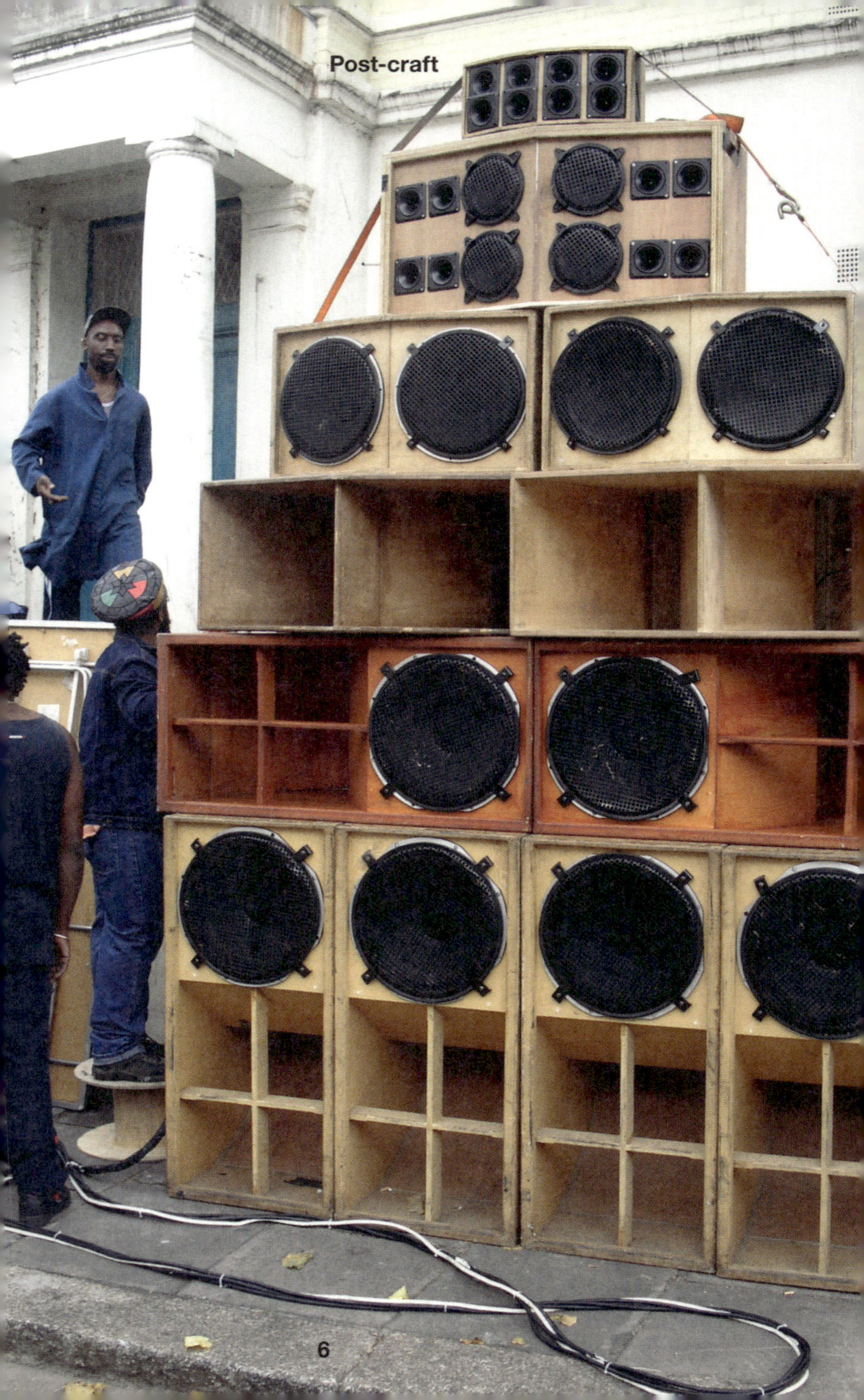

WALLPAPER WALLPAPER WALLPAPER THE WORLD THE WORLD THE WORLD THE WORLD THE WORLD

JEREMY DELLER & ALEX COLES

Jeremy Deller interviewed by Alex Coles

Alex Coles: There are a number of ways your work touches on notions of craft – some more directly than others. The most obvious being your engagement with the figure of William Morris, who was central to "English Magic" – your Venice Biennale British Pavilion commission in 2013 – and the exhibition you curated in 2014/15 at Modern Art Oxford, which placed him alongside Andy Warhol. Where does your interest in him stem from?

Jeremy Deller: Morris is such an important figure, and his influence is so huge that it often seems invisible. First there is the broad scope of his work; then there is his interest in reproduction and commitment to circulating his work using the broadest possible distribution channels. In a way, Morris wanted to wallpaper the world. Ideas of visibility, publishing, reproduction, printing, and the notion of a practice that couldn't be defined easily – if at all – underpinned his work. There's a sense of Morris being some kind of prophet, pointing the way for future generations. He's had a huge influence, but so often it's under the surface.

AC: Why did you choose Morris as a subject when representing Britain at the Venice Biennale?

JD: I liked the fact that I was occupying the pavilion that represented the country Morris came from, and also that he knew Venice and had spent time there with John Ruskin. Both of them would have been disgusted at the wealth on display during the biennale. The idea of Morris the socialist returning to Venice as a giant who destroys Russian oligarch Roman Abramovich's yacht moored outside the Giardini during the 2011 biennale was extremely appealing. Did you see the yacht?

AC: No.

Page 6:

Jeremy Deller with Alan Kane, *Folk Archive*, 2005. Speaker Stack, Notting Hill Carnival, London, 2003.

JD: It literally overshadowed everything, assuming a significant place in people's consciousness. During the opening week, it was the only thing being talked about, and I just had to use it as the centerpiece of my exhibition for the next biennale.

AC: The installation also contextualized the image in a very specific way: alongside the mural was a series of documents and certificates attesting to the change in ownership of businesses and properties in Russia, many of which were manipulated so they would fall into the hands of syndicates controlled by oligarchs like Abramovich after the Berlin Wall came down.

JD: Exactly. In a way you could see that room as an epic tale where Morris is the beginning of socialist idealism, in the United Kingdom at least, and Abramovich is the end of communism. Visitors could also take away a poster of the image, in reference to the tradition of English aristocracy visiting Venice on the Grand Tour and leaving with a drawing or painting depicting a scene in Venice. Because of this, the image was more widely circulated. There is a poetic justice in "English Magic" that I like.

AC: Who actually painted the mural of Morris and the yacht?

JD: It was Stuart Hughes, who does a lot of airbrush work and actually painted a motorbike for Abramovich at some point, apparently. He usually works in miniature, but likes working on big things too.

AC: In this sense it's almost like craft is embedded in the process of production of the mural.

JD: Right, but I use many different craftsmen across the production of my work, so it's not

“WHENEVER PEOPLE CIVILIZATIONS GET DEGENERATE MATERIALISTIC

THEY AL POINT THEIR OUT BEAUTY RICHES...”

unusual. There wasn't a deliberate point being made there.

AC: With his initiating the Arts & Crafts movement, the overtly aestheticized part of Morris's project is the most widely known: the beautiful fabrics, the woodcuts, and so on. As your research deepened, did you find this problematic?

JD: The aspects of his practice you mention represent great beauty. Morris was quite a character, with extreme beliefs about aesthetics, politics, and the place of art in society. That's what's so interesting about him: he made these objects of great beauty but he was also a very political person. Morris wanted to return a sense of dignity and worth to labor and craft. Today Morris's designs appear very middle class, but he was a great follower of Karl Marx, who was living in London at the same time. I don't think they met, but Morris was one of the first people to set up a socialist party in London, giving lectures about socialism that focused on the working man's role in society, the dignity of work, and the exploitative aspects of the factory system.

AC: At this point, were you starting to work on "Love Is Enough: William Morris and Andy Warhol"?

JD: No, that came later, and I approached it in a very different way. The title, "Love Is Enough," came from one of Morris's books and of course sounds a bit like something Warhol could have said. During the run-up to the exhibition, there was a staged dialogue with Warhol and Morris specialists and me. I read out quotes like, "Whenever people and civilizations get degenerate and materialistic, they always point at their outward beauty and riches," and asked the specialists whom they attributed the quote to.

AND

From Andy Warhol, *The Philosophy of Andy Warhol (From A to B and Back Again)* (New York: Harcourt, 1975).

AND

VAYS
AT
ARD
AND

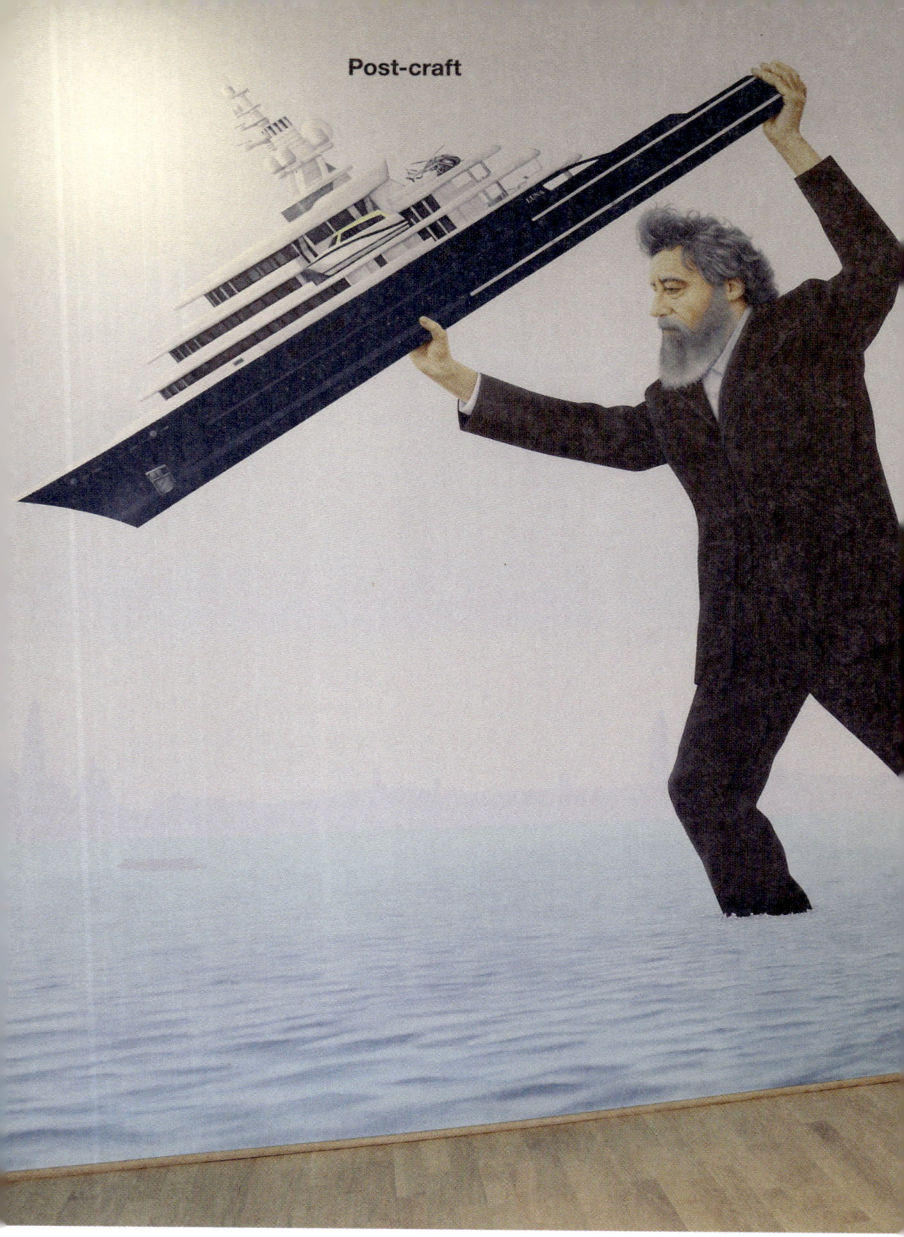

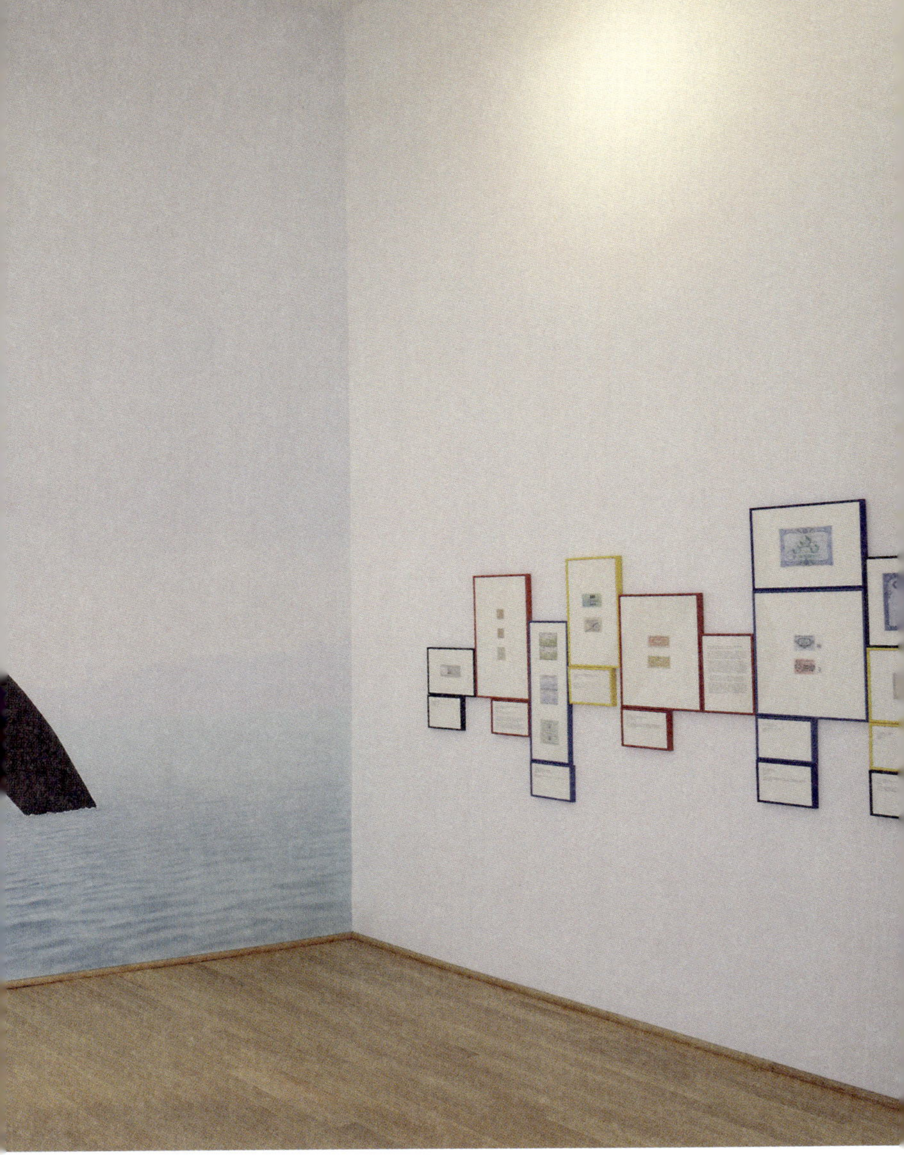

Jeremy Deller, "English Magic," British Pavilion, 55th Venice Biennale, 2013. Installation view. Photo by Christiano Corte.

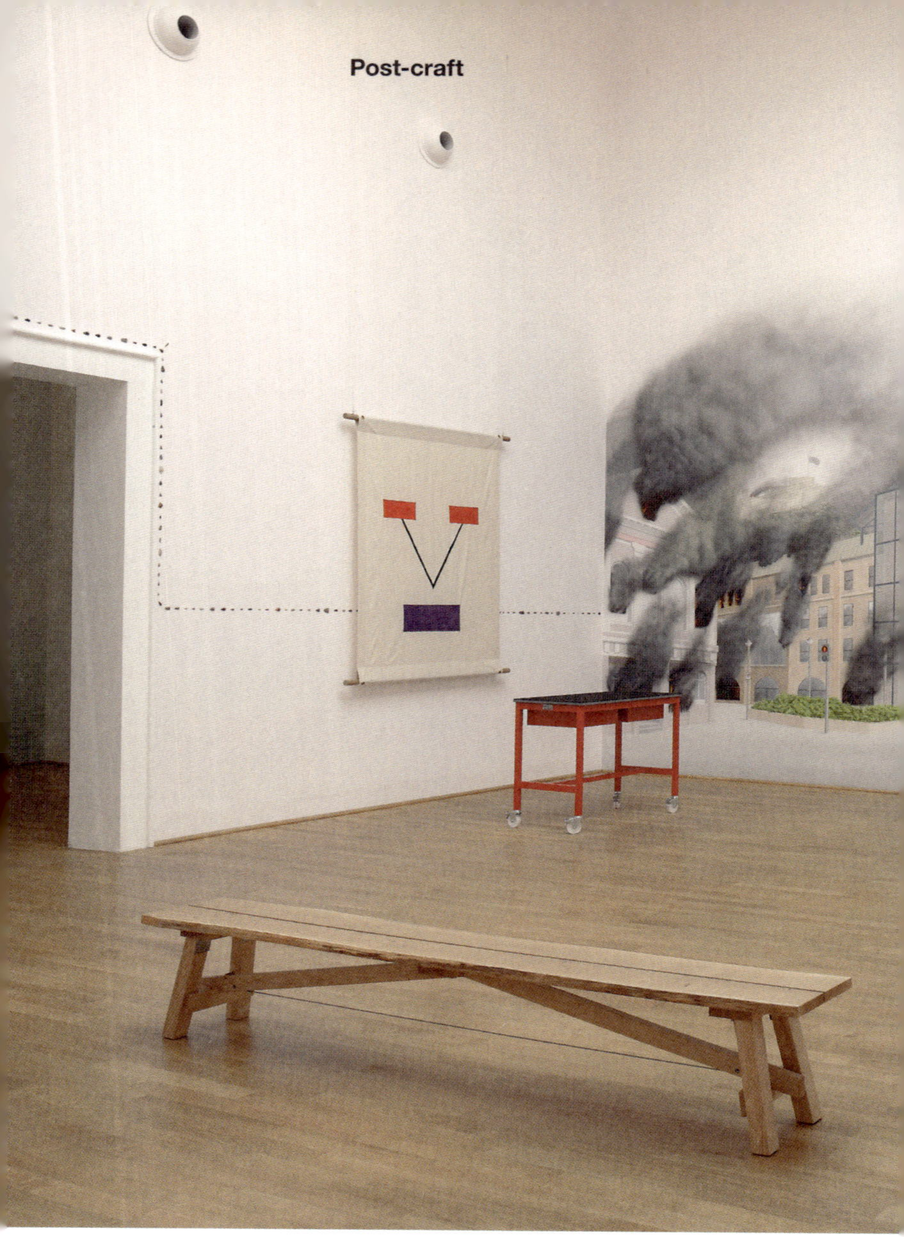

Jeremy Deller, "English Magic," British Pavilion, 55th Venice Biennale, 2013. Installation view. Photo by Christiano Corte.

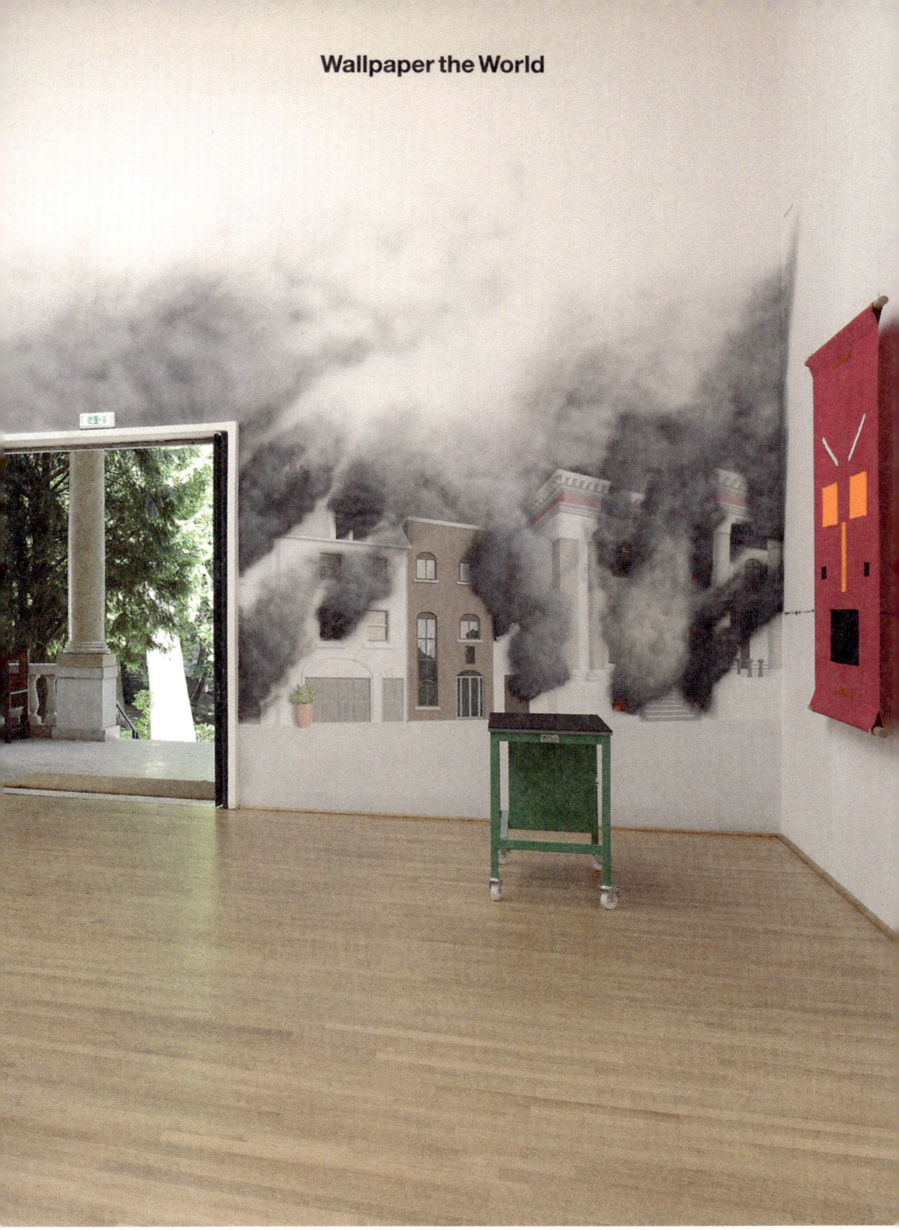

AC: Did the panel guess correctly?

JD: No, almost every time they got it wrong, which was great of course because it gave purpose to the exhibition's premise. The quote I just mentioned was, for instance, by Warhol, but in tone and content it's very near to things Morris wrote.

"Love Is Enough" revolved around core themes such as the mass popularization of contemporary art, design processes and manufacturing techniques, shared mythologies and obsessions, and politics and publications. So in one room, Morris's *Holy Grail* tapestries (1890), which depict scenes from the legend of King Arthur, were placed alongside Warhol's *Flash* portfolio of eleven screen prints (1968) made with images that document the aftermath of John F. Kennedy's assassination. The heroism celebrated in the Camelot stories is linked to the tragedy of the Kennedy family told through the portraits. A range of vintage *Interview* magazines displayed revealed Warhol's taste for high-impact design and candid celebrity conversations. This is contrasted with Morris's interest in medieval legends and iconography, shared with artists like Dante Gabriel Rossetti and Edward Burne-Jones. Rosetti's and Burne-Jones's interest in the politics of their times is echoed in screen prints by Warhol of newspaper cuttings on current affairs. Alongside the prints were Morris's socialist writings and speeches, including items such as Morris's own membership card for the socialist league – a nice detail.

AC: Do you think Morris gave an artist like Warhol permission to move across so many fields and mediums?

JD: Yes. In a way, Morris is the first multimedia artist, working across every available field.

Now we'd say he had a multimedia empire. Without him it would have been much more difficult to understand a figure like Warhol. The other thing of course is that they both developed their own publishing platforms – and this is key to what they wanted to say and how they said it.

AC: What was it like when you visited Warhol's Factory, which was located close to *Interview*'s headquarters, at such a foundational stage in your intellectual development?

JD: I never saw Warhol actually paint or print in the Factory, but spending time at *Interview* magazine was interesting. Seeing all of this at a young age was a particularly formative experience for me. To have then been able to visit Morris's multiple workshops, studios, houses, offices – all of which he operated across – would have been even more amazing!

AC: How did you come into contact with Warhol?

JD: I introduced myself to him when he visited London in 1986 and, along with a friend, was invited to his hotel suite to meet his entourage. Eventually this led to an invite to visit the Factory. When I went to New York and saw how it worked, I just thought it was amazing. I was only twenty, so I wasn't really sure what I was going to do in the future, but the experience made the art history I was studying at the Courtauld Institute look very boring.

AC: Given your passion for Warhol and Morris, are you in a way attempting to position your own practice by making, or articulating, this parallel between them?

JD: How do you mean?

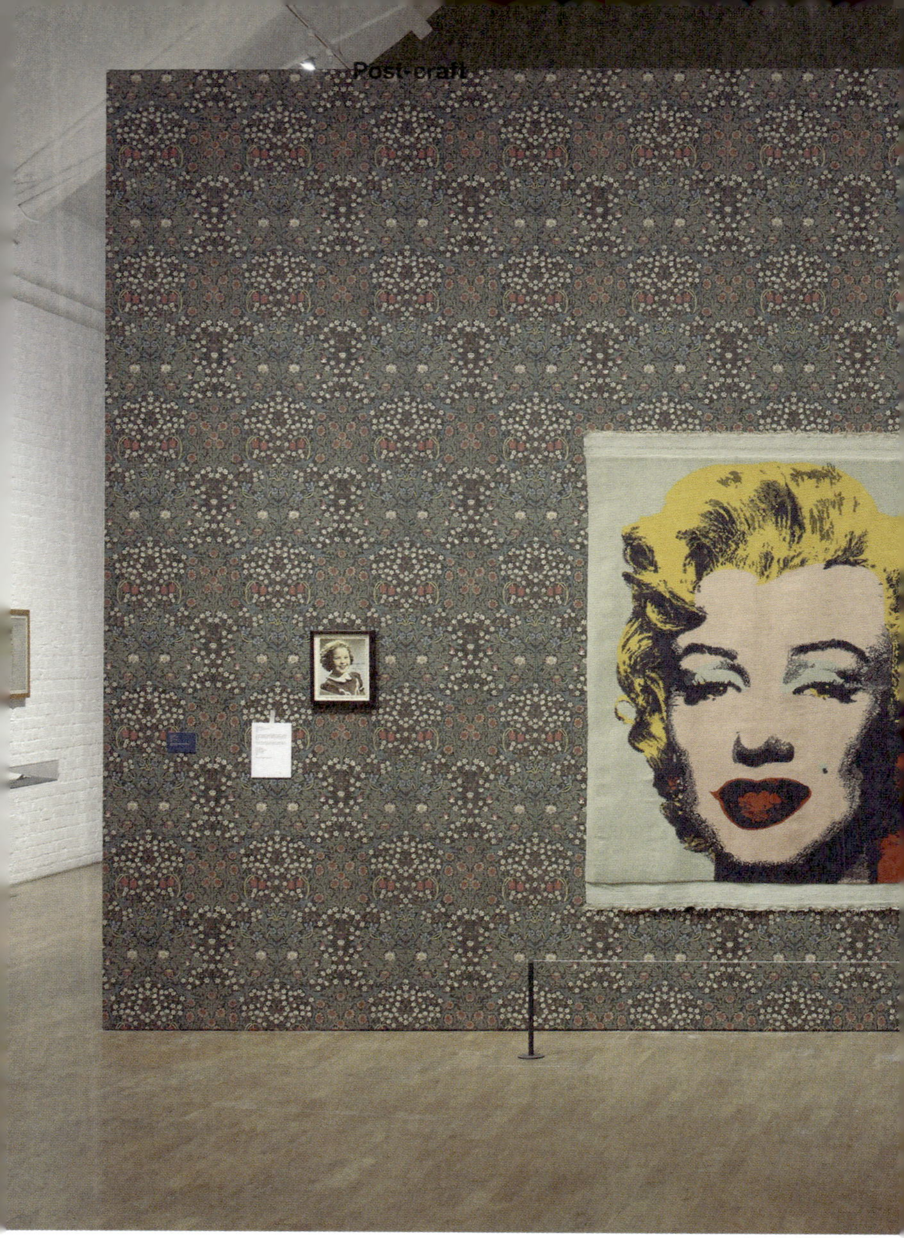

"Love Is Enough: William Morris & Andy Warhol," curated by Jeremy Deller, Modern Art Oxford, 2014–15. Exhibition view.

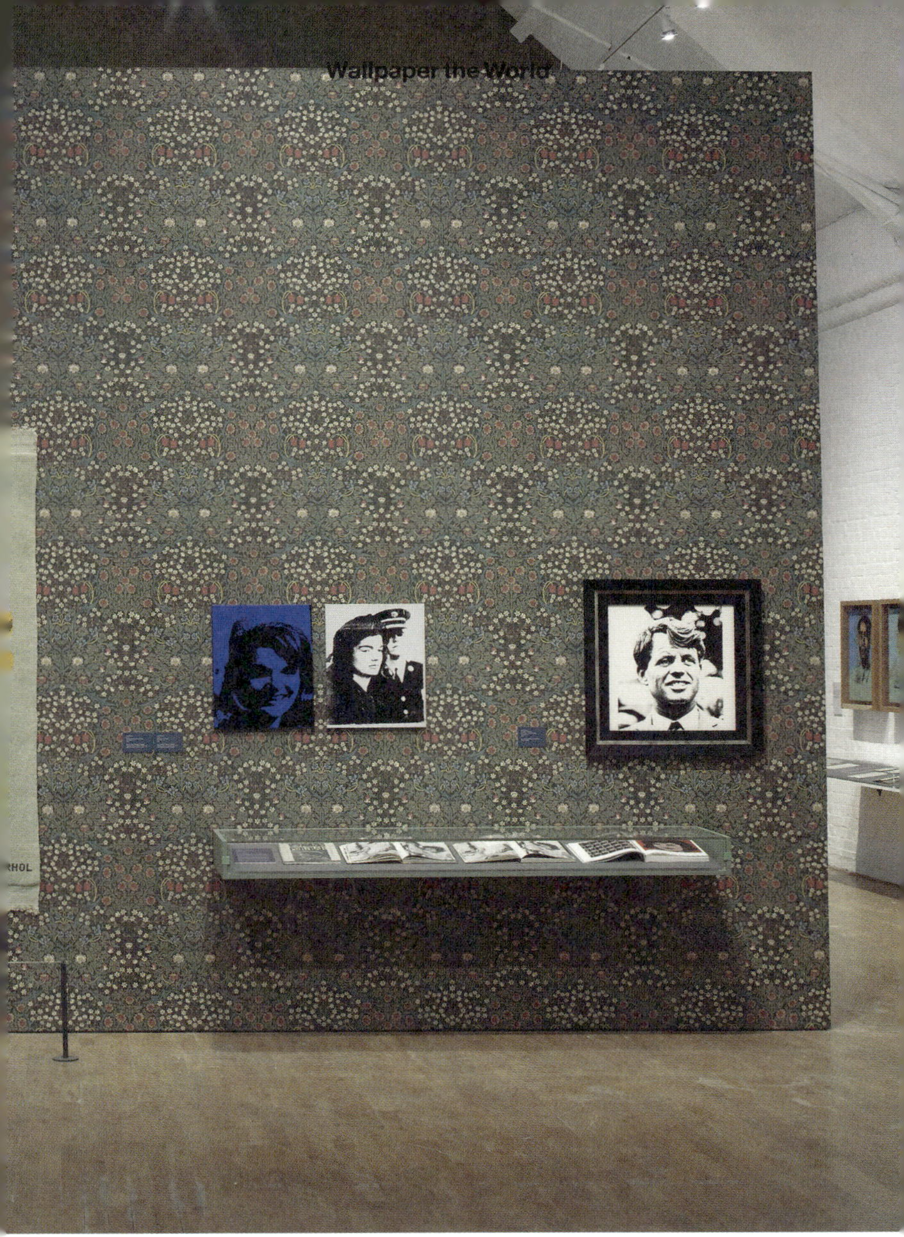
Wallpaper the World

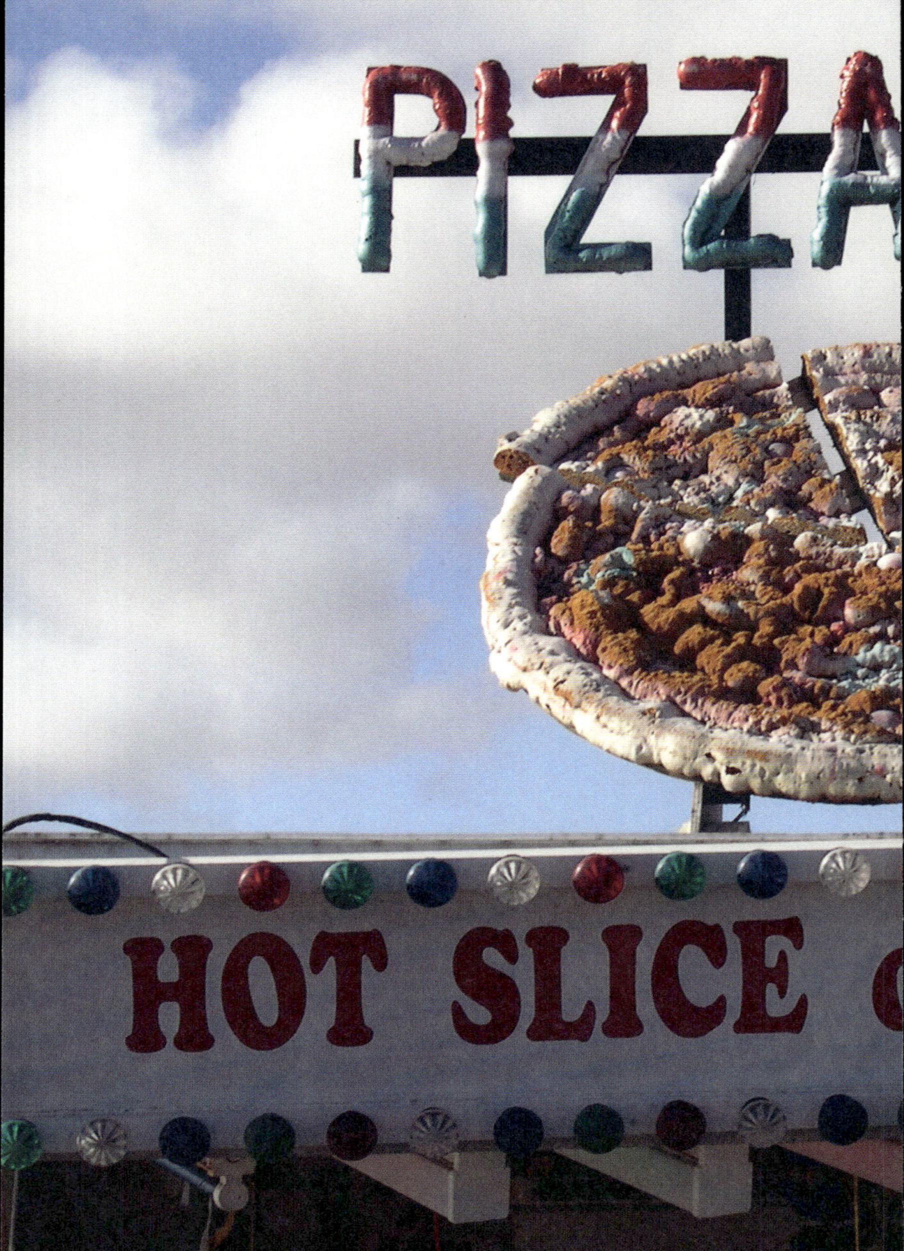
PIZZA
HOT SLICE

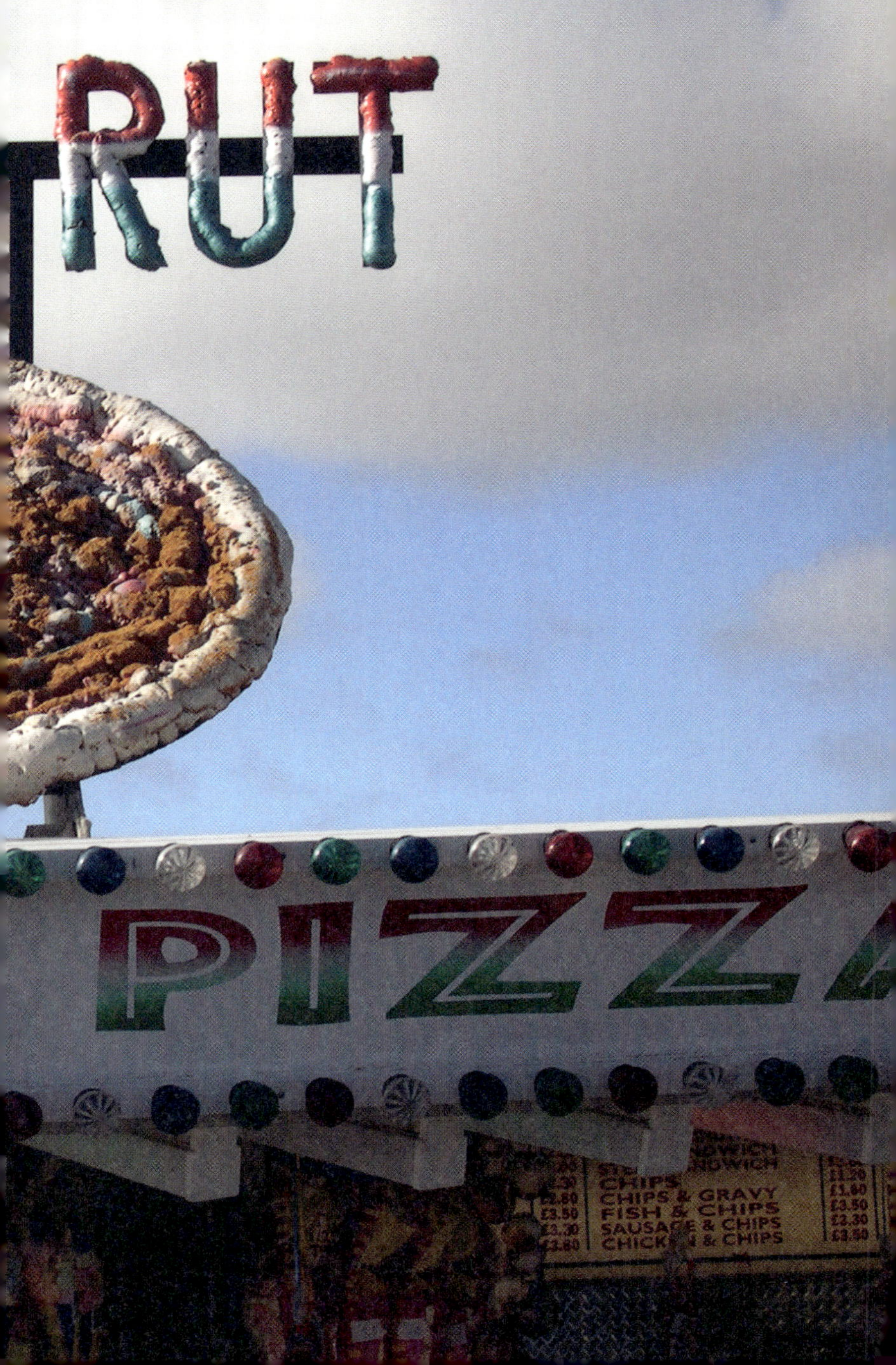
RUT
PIZZ
CHIPS
CHIPS & GRAVY
FISH & CHIPS

AC: In the sense that even though we are much closer to the era of Warhol than that of Morris, your work takes elements from both and retools them: we get Morris's interest in social injustice with *The Battle of Orgreave* (2001) and Warhol's attraction to the culture of celebrity with *The Search for Bez* (1994).

JD: I see what you mean – maybe, but never in a conscious way.

AC: Warhol was also fascinated with the language of the vernacular, not only in the iconic works but also with his *Time Capsules* (1974–87), in which thousands of his everyday possessions where consigned into numbered cardboard boxes. For *Folk Archive* (2005), coproduced with Alan Kane, you collected an array of objects engaging with subjects from British popular culture, such as gurning competitions, Morris dancing, and political demonstrations. What was behind this work?

JD: I have always been interested in forms of artistic production taking place outside the art world, where everyday life and craft meet. This is what *Folk Archive* is about. If you like art, you should like most art and not only that made by professional artists. If a child makes something, I'm interested; and if Caravaggio makes something, I'm interested. Craft is present in both.

Pages 20–21:

Jeremy Deller with Alan Kane, *Folk Archive*, 2005. Pizza Rut, Blackpool, Lancashire.

CRAFTY CRAFTY CRAFTY CRAFTY RATHER THAN CRAFTED CRAFTED CRAFTED

ASSEMBLE & 6A

Maria Lisogorskaya from Assemble and Tom Emerson from 6a in conversation with Catharine Rossi

Catharine Rossi: How do you both know each other?

Maria Lisogorskaya: I was in Tom's unit in third year at the University of Cambridge, and I guess that's how a lot of people in Assemble know him.

Tom Emerson: We met in 2007/8.

CR: And you were teaching a particular unit at Cambridge?

TE: Yes, the students did a third-year project, which was to redesign the Ruskin School of Art in Oxford. Richard Wentworth, then its head, had asked me to do it some years previously, but I was always slightly uncomfortable with this idea of Cambridge students meeting Oxford students and putting the world to rights. But somehow that year it seemed to fit, and the meeting of all these people happened within Richard's orbit, lending it a certain temperament that encouraged people to work beyond their given predispositions. It's interesting that Assemble later responded to that moment and context in a way that I hadn't seen before. It may have been the recession – the architectural profession was in a kind of malaise. At a practical level, there was no work, and at an emotional level, it just didn't feel that the whole system was right. That's what it seemed like to me, even though I come from a much more conventional architectural practice, where we are commissioned to design architecture that is fabricated by other people.

ML: When I graduated, we did the EXYZT Lido in Southwark, part of the Union Street temporary project. That was interesting because it was the first time we built on-site. At university, I found it difficult to understand the separation between how things are designed and how they are made. There was a real disconnect between the drawings and details students worked on and the world around us. But then when I was building on-site, it started to make more sense.

TE: That disconnect has always been there, but I think it was felt more when the professionalized system seemed to have failed and what was going on outside the professional structure seemed to offer many more possibilities.

CR: For Assemble, making was an outlet for a criticism of the status quo in architecture?

ML: Yes, in a way. It varies between members of Assemble, but there's a general desire to have more fun with architecture and design. After graduating from university, people went into jobs where you were exclusively working in one part of the process as opposed to having a more holistic view of each project. This led to a desire to do something from start to finish: get it done, build it, and really feel the materials. Cineroleum, a temporary cinema built on a derelict petrol station, was perhaps the first project to do this.

CR: Cineroleum was quite an experience. I can't remember what film I watched, but I do remember the curtain coming up at the end; the sense of heightening a different relationship with an urban environment was quite acute. Like much of your work, it goes against the grain of static, image-friendly architecture and design that's so well suited to image-based web platforms like *Dezeen*.

ML: Both Cineroleum and Folly for a Flyover, a motorway-undercroft-turned-arts-space, were extremely difficult to record and describe because they're so performative. In a way you had to be there to get it.

CR: There's a kind of fetishization the crafted, or the process of making, can induce that is resisted if you don't document it. In this sense, what is your relationship with craft and making?

ML: Craft is a loaded word. Making is something we enjoy and that helps us develop a project. Recently Adam Willis and Paloma Strelitz developed a special facade element for Goldsmiths Centre for Contemporary Art, and he did a few 1:1 tests to be developed into a product. That's one side of it. But then we've obviously made some buildings ourselves, and I've made things like tiles. Even though I frequently use making as a way of designing or developing a project, Adam is the only person I could say is really a craftsperson. Sometimes we've learned a new skill to deliver a project. For Cineroleum, we received a lot of advice from theater chandlers and riggers. To my mind, craft refers to something that you develop over the years from doing the same thing over and over.

CR: What do you think it is that making offers as an approach?

ML: It brings you back to the reality of materials and how they come together – it lets you experiment beyond a drawing. If you only draw what a tile is going to be, you can only use what you've seen before or something in your imagination, neither of which probably relates to how it's actually made. The process of making allows you to feel out what's possible. In this sense, making is designing.

CR: Who builds Assemble's architecture?

ML: A range of people: standard contractors, carpenters, artists, and us. It depends on the project.

TE: I guess I share Maria's slight discomfort with the word craft because it can evoke all sorts of slightly worthy, self-righteous, ethical virtues. Maria's already talked about making. I like the word skill because it goes from the invisible to the very visible. Like a potter or a ceramicist, a plumber can also be really skillful.

TE: Even John Ruskin and William Morris seem to be somehow trendy again. In *The Map and the Territory* (2010), Michel Houellebecq has this strange conversation with Morris. The whole journey narrated in the book is about trying to reexamine the idea of making, because it's all about the objects of industry, map-making, and portraiture. This return of craft is not necessarily taking place within the same political or even aesthetic traditions of the past. Certainly in Houellebecq's hands it's a bit nasty, and somehow approaches like his make it feel quite fresh.

CR: That's one of the interesting tensions. Craft has always been problematic, if not slightly unpopular. But now that it has become popular, craft is causing discomfort in a different kind of way.

TE: Partly that's because of the way it's been so readily appropriated by the market. Craft is so ubiquitous, whether it takes the form of beer, clothes, coffee, food, or bicycles. It's very difficult to feel any warmth toward something that's been so broadly appropriated.

ML: It's an illusion to imply people are not part of this messy, industrialized world full of crap, and instead live in a bubble where only beautiful things exist.

TE: The notion of craft has become divided.

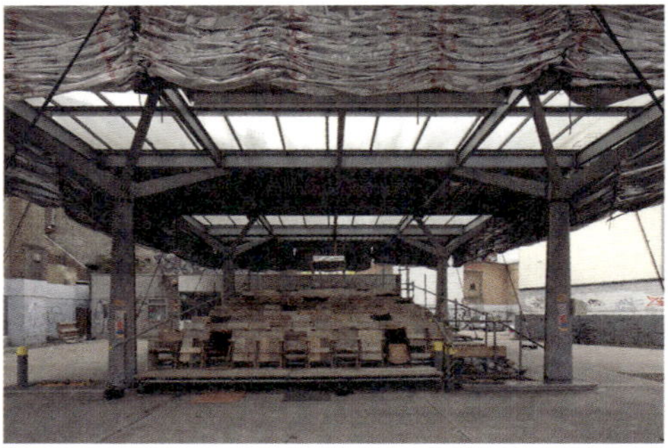

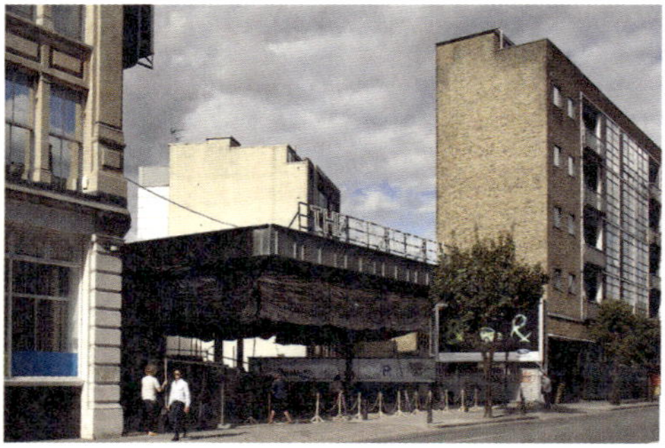

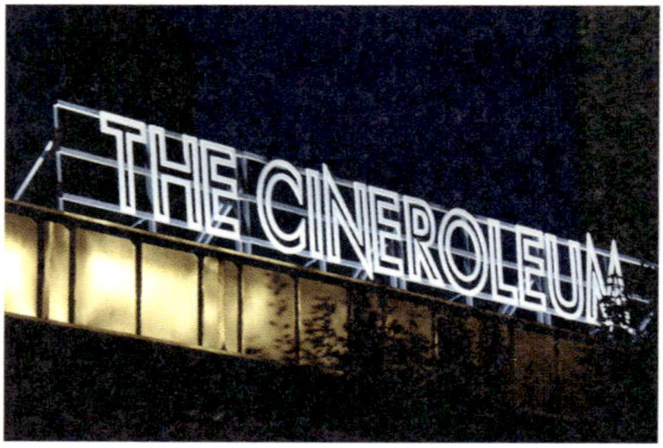

Assemble, Cineroleum,
London, 2010.

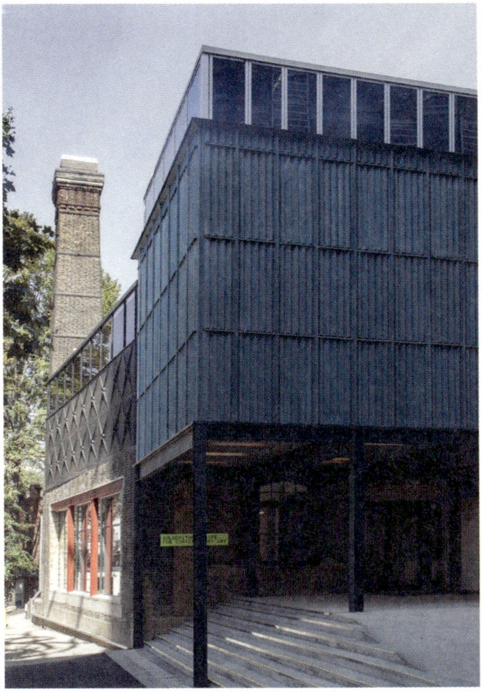

Assemble, exterior
of Goldsmiths Centre
for Contemporary Art,
London, 2018.

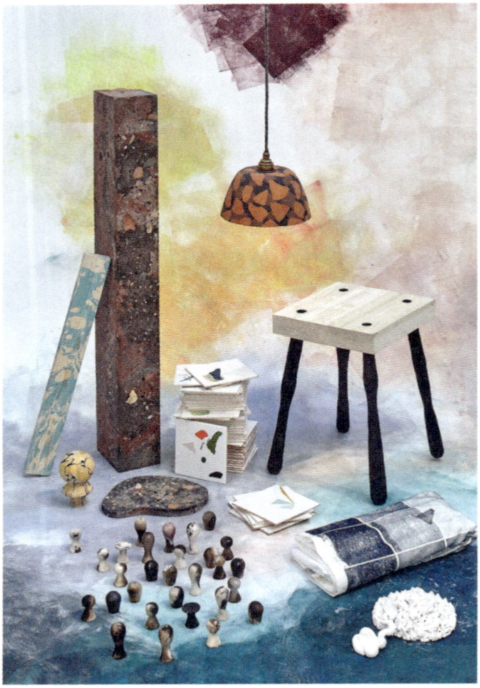

Assemble/Granby Workshop, Liverpool, 2015.

Assemble, Granby Workshop, Liverpool, 2015. Photo by Rob Battersby.

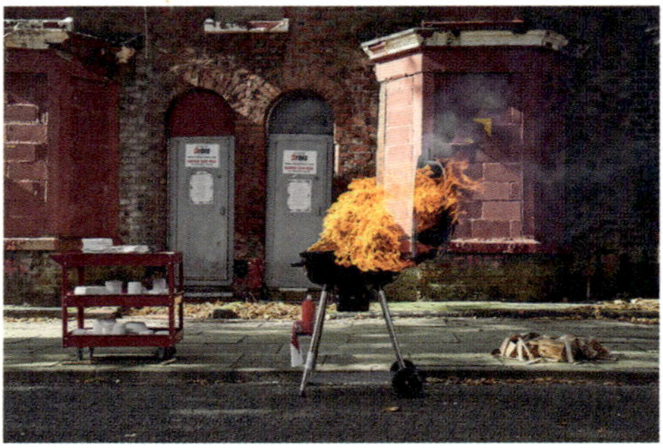

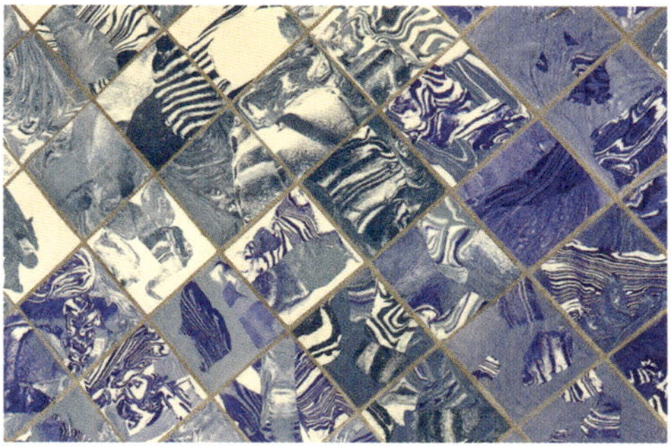

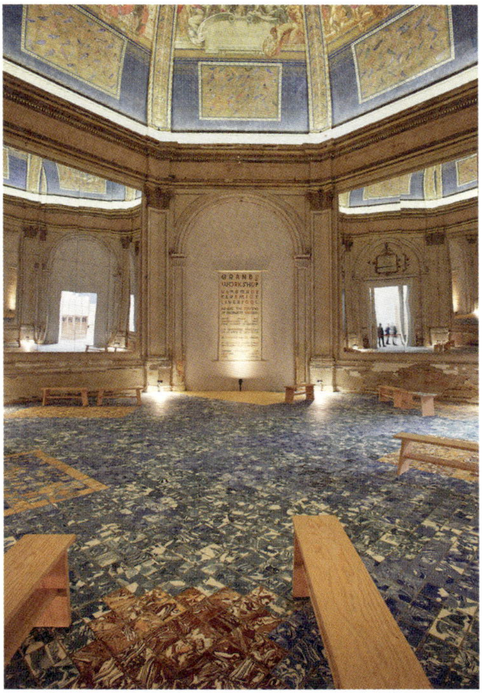

Assemble/Granby Workshop, *The Factory Floor*, Venice Biennale, 2018.

The aspects of it to do with skill and the way knowledge is passed on – the whole idea of an evolution of the field of applied knowledge – is very engaging. But then it is also taken to these other places and then you think, I'd rather keep my distance …

Do you know Richard Artschwager? Artschwager produced well-crafted furniture and then became not quite a Pop artist, not really a Conceptual artist, and not really a Minimalist, but he was somewhere in that soup of sixties art. One of the reasons I'm interested in him is that he used craft to subvert craft. Yesterday I was reading an essay in which Artschwager explains why he swapped natural wood for Formica: "Formica the great ugly material, the horror of its age, which I think I liked suddenly because I was sick of all this beautiful wood."

CR: That's like Ettore Sottsass's underlying strategy: you use a thing against itself, and visibly so. Maria, could you talk a bit about what the place of craft is in Assemble?

ML: The non-craft aspect of craft I can. We don't really spend a long-enough time on one particular process to really make it perfect. But we do experiment with different ways of making. In one instance, we cast concrete and experimented with different aggregates and surfaces, making furniture and cladding. In this sense, we've developed skills by using and developing a technique that's led to its misuse.

TE: It's more like inquiry than craft?

ML: Exactly. That's a good way of putting it.

CR: But the aesthetic in your work seems to be quite conscious or conscientiously handmade.

It's got an unevenness that is only possible because of human intervention.

ML: Yeah. It's funny because with the Granby Workshop, a social enterprise in Liverpool (and part of the larger Granby Four Streets project) that very much started with handmade processes, the whole idea was to develop accessible techniques that are cheap and speedy and don't require much technology or investment. Now we're trying to make it into a business. We want to maintain this sense of an enjoyable working environment where the person fabricating is making the same thing, but with a degree of variety so that it stays interesting. Because we also want to make it more efficient, we're starting to use industrial machines like an extruder, which you'd use for making bricks, but then tampering with these machines to introduce variety and play.

TE: What you're describing has to do with the economy of a particular work or project, and identifying or even developing a technology that matches that economy. I don't think 6a had thought about doing really fancy decorative cast facades until the Paul Smith shop-front commission on Albemarle Street in Mayfair. This is like, really, every square centimeter of this ground is worth a fortune, whereas the work we're doing now is much more industrial.

CR: Can you give an example?

TE: The project for MK Gallery in Milton Keynes has a steel-framed box with steel cladding on the outside. It's brutally efficient: a grid on the outside and a grid in plan. With its scale it has got a tougher economy to it, and in some respects it is a world away from Paul Smith.

But in other respects it's quite similar, because essentially it's cladding, just cheaper and bigger.

CR: As economies of scale change, how does the viability of making – and the notion of craft – change for you both?

ML: The question of scale is important. We're not working in the same way as before. Now we don't make everything; we don't make popcorn anymore, unfortunately. So I think we're just trying to identify the best opportunities to make a difference. It's about finding an interesting material supply and turning a given situation around. Sometimes it's about making facades, sometimes it's about something completely different. I mean, I can't really predict what we're going to do next, but being more critical of our own value and what we bring to a project is something we're trying to do. It may completely change, but at the moment there is a definite interest in making and materiality that is likely to continue – even if that means making samples for something someone else makes later – because it's still a way of designing through making.

CR: But also in the way you think about how you facilitate making both within your own individual projects – like Granby – but also studios such as the one we are speaking in, where you make facilities for communities of makers.

ML: Yeah, and I think that definitely has a political side as well. Spaces like the Blackhorse Workshop are vital to the discussion around industry and the urban environment, trying to provide places in the city that are messy and where noise can be made. The term workshop instead of studio is key here, especially now that developers have started to retail studios that are just white rooms where you have to leave by six.

TE: One of the things related to notion of making and craft that we haven't talked about, but that plays a vital role in both our practices, is bricolage. Like craft it is also slightly contaminated. There's more to it than a form of junkyard chic. I understand it to be much more about dealing imaginatively with the situation around you. That may involve self-building or setting up a local enterprise. Both are equally forms of bricolage and about adapting to the situation you are in. Colin Rowe describes Rome as being the ultimate bricolage city: the mashing together of temples and bars and markets to form an accidental but rich composition.

CR: So, it's about an attitude?

TE: Yes, an attitude that can be applied to a whole city or a certain approach to making. Bricolage sits somewhat easier with me than the notion of craft. I also really like the idea of the gardener, and with it the idea of maintenance and care. When you produce something, it's just the beginning: you have to be super patient and caring to ensure something grows. In one sense the idea of the gardener is literal – a lot of projects have been structured around landscape ideas – but it also has a metaphorical dimension, in the sense that it places greater significance on how things are operated and used.

CR: But then architecture kind of induces that. There's this idea that the architect creates scenes and settings for people to exist in and maintain. Craftsmanship is present in the scenes and stages you create.

TE: Yes, and this returns us to the notion of making: by being interested in making you somehow get a little bit closer to the user. This is the complete opposite of the ongoing

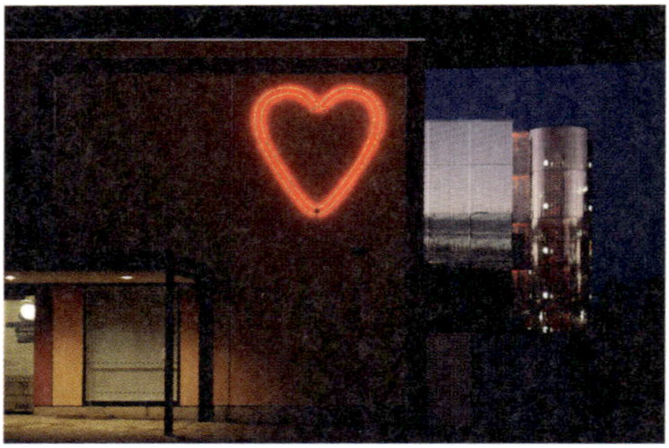

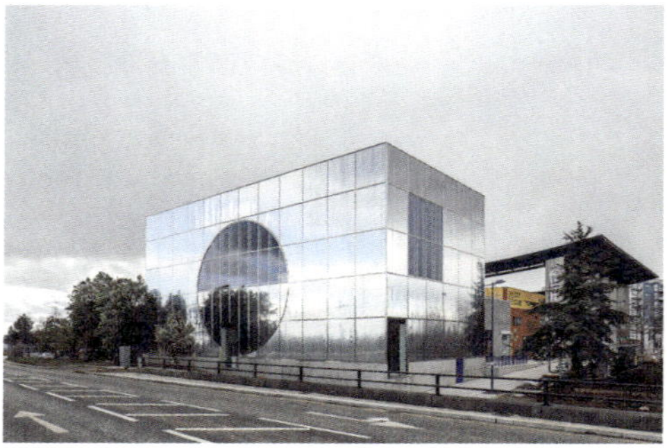

6a architects, MK Gallery exterior, Milton Keynes, 2019.

6a architects, MK Gallery exterior, Milton Keynes, 2019, featuring *City Club* by Gareth Jones and Nils Norman. Photo by Johan Dehlin.

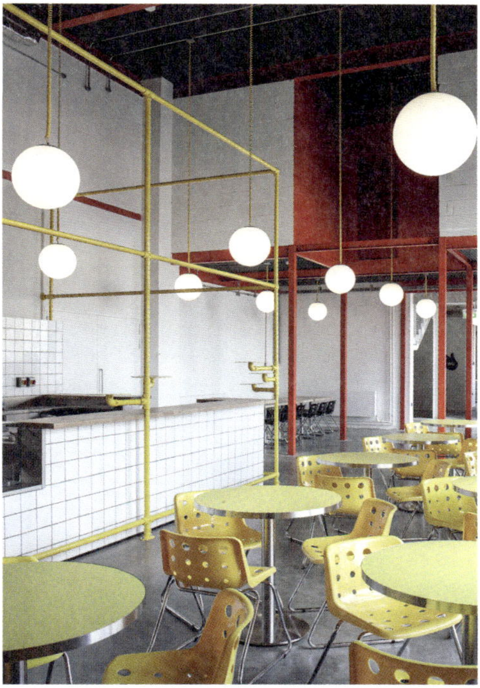

6a architects, MK Gallery interior, Milton Keynes, 2019, featuring *City Club* by Gareth Jones and Nils Norman. Photo by Johan Dehlin.

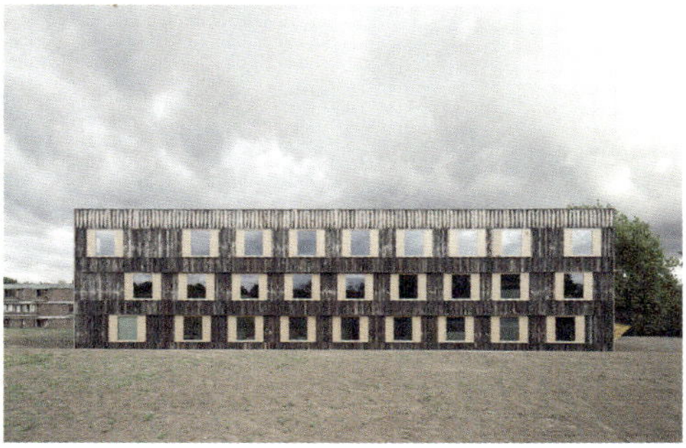

6a architects, Cowan Court, Churchill College, University of Cambridge, 2019. Photo by Johan Dehlin.

population of the field by consultants. It's a very weird notion. Like the famous Henry Ford quote, "If I'd asked my customers what they wanted, they would have said a slightly faster horse." If you're going to try and be innovative or progressive, sometimes you have to do things that people don't expect, that they don't ask for. But that gets us a long way from craft.

CR: Not necessarily. It does bring us to the role that craft has played in the public reception of your work. Discussions around craft fed into your success with the Turner Prize because art has used craft as a convenient way of rebelling against some of its own boundaries. Previous Turner Prize winner Grayson Perry comes to mind.

ML: Yes, I guess there was a narrative in play about usefulness and the arts and crafts. The discussion was centered on the idea of trying to bring art back to a place where it can be detached from the abstract world it's been locked in and accessed by a different audience. But this was not something we were really in control of – it was more projected onto us. While it's provided us with a range of opportunities, I don't think we ever meant for that to happen.

TE: Viewing it from the outside makes it somewhat easier to analyze. Obviously when you won the Turner Prize, there was a lot of chatter. Was it right? Was it not right? At the same time there was also a general acknowledgment that somehow contemporary art had got itself into a bit of a knot, and that Assemble provided one way of undoing it. While it was difficult to categorize in terms of discipline, many were convinced by the sincerity of their spirit. Suddenly there was something that was outwardly facing in a very hermetic world.

CR: How does this relate back to the role of craft?

TE: You don't correct someone when they say your work is well crafted. It's usually meant as a compliment, even if sometimes it makes you slightly uncomfortable. If someone says that something is well crafted, it's another way of saying it's well made. Possibly it's a way of saying it's well designed too. So perhaps the term well crafted shouldn't always bring such a high degree of discomfort. It's just that at a critical level, craft has always occupied a very contentious place. It doesn't have a sound critical discourse associated with it the way architecture and contemporary art do. Peter Dormer was the first person I read that pointed this out.

CR: Yes, and he's key to this publication and the whole notion of post-craft. During our conversation we've talked a lot about craft, but is there any last statements you would like to make? Is that the most you've ever spoken about craft in one go?

TE: Yes, but one thing I like that I haven't mentioned is the idea of being crafty – someone who's crafty is not entirely to be trusted. Ultimately, I'd rather be crafty than crafted.

ML: Yes, me too!

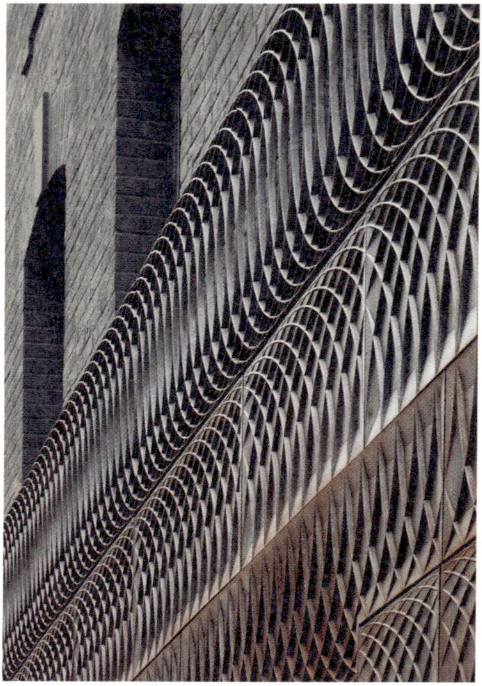

6a architects, facade of
Paul Smith store, Mayfair,
London, 2013.

THE POST-CRAFT TURN TURN TURN

MARTINA MARGETTS

TURN

TURN

TURN

1/ Cited in Sarah Archer, "The Meaning of Clay at the Whitney Biennial," *Hypoallergic*, April 24, 2014, https://hyperallergic.com/122270/the-meaning-of-clay-at-the-whitney-biennial/.

Decoding

Craft is always essential to being human: our need to clothe, feed, relate, move about, and experience life and culture remains constant, but the products and agency of our making now look and function differently. Post-craft may simply indicate the progressively fluid parameters of things and daily life, or a shift from things to experiences, from production to service industries, or from the tangible to the virtual. It may connote a fragmenting of disciplines and identities or a new definition of making because of key shifts in the nature of human and artificial intelligences.

Post-craft flourishes in the current creative and sociopolitical condition of flux. Objects, disciplines, and territories have been decentered. Archetypes of craft practice endure – in particular the central role assumed by the vessel in ceramics – but their appraisal is premised differently. Gone is the cultish allegiance to Bernard Leach's concept of the absolute standard, which guided makers to provide objects aimed to please aesthetically and embody a moral integrity and humility through the process. Sterling Ruby's "Basin Theology" (2013), a series of three clay vessels that was included in the 2014 Whitney Biennial in New York, was a deceptively ugly and unskilled new vessel form. In describing the rationale behind her eclectic selection for the biennial more generally, curator Michelle Grabner compared it to "building a curriculum: every tradition and technique gets a voice."[1] A celebration of sloppiness underlines the libertarianism of our time. There is no fixed yardstick of either aesthetic or ethical judgment. Rather, there is the task of reconciling differences, which is achieved through intersectionality in creative practice and everyday life.

The building of a curriculum that Grabner proposes resynthesizes art, craft, design, and architecture. This has beneficially enfranchised craft practices within the continual shape-shift of visual culture and the present era of climate change and environmental uncertainty, from deconstructivist architecture's reconfiguration of form and space in the built environment to the cycles of life and death that appear in the work of the YBAs. Both autonomous craft and "applied arts" practices have a stake in these issues of environments and functions. Visual-culture theories are inevitably absorbed. New materialism, object-oriented ontology, and affect theory, which were developed through thinkers such as Jane Bennett, Diana Coole, Timothy Morton, and Graham Harman, deepen insight into the conditions of visual culture by which craft is currently appraised.

Harman's philosophical insight has emphasized each object's singular significance as an entity in the world that has meaning as a thing in itself and in relation to other objects, and not just as a transitional and transactional object between humans.[2] This explains the popular fascination with the presence of objects in terms of material and technique, composition and decomposition, and their object relations. The conversation between objects is explored in installations by cross-media artists such as Helen Marten and Ryan Gander, which speak of the networks connecting to a wider social experience of daily life as theorized by Bruno Latour. It is a post-craft language of interconnectedness and interaction, as opposed to autonomy and essentialism. Phoebe Cummings further examines this relational language, enabling her materials to question the value in things by asserting, through her hand-built, raw-clay landscapes, the transience of being, becoming, and disintegration. Contingency and uncertainty characterize the post-craft condition. So, too, does ambiguity. Emma Woffenden's tricky encounters with the body are played out as staged dramas of full-sized glass figures with props made of wood, metal, and rubber. A cross-disciplinary relation between sciences and arts has focused on the idea of the experiment, a speculative approach to cause and effect, evidenced in Keith Harrison's electrical combustions for his 2012–13 residency at the Victoria & Albert Museum and in the 2014 project "Parallel Practices" at King's College London, where makers worked with biomedical scientists. Alexandra Daisy Ginsberg is the quintessential post-craft practitioner. She describes herself as an artist, designer, and writer who uses synthetic biology to explore nature, science, and technology, and who works with "scientists, engineers, artists, designers, social scientists, museums,

2/ Graham Harman, *Tool-Being: Heidegger and the Metaphysics of Objects* (Chicago: Open Court, 2002).

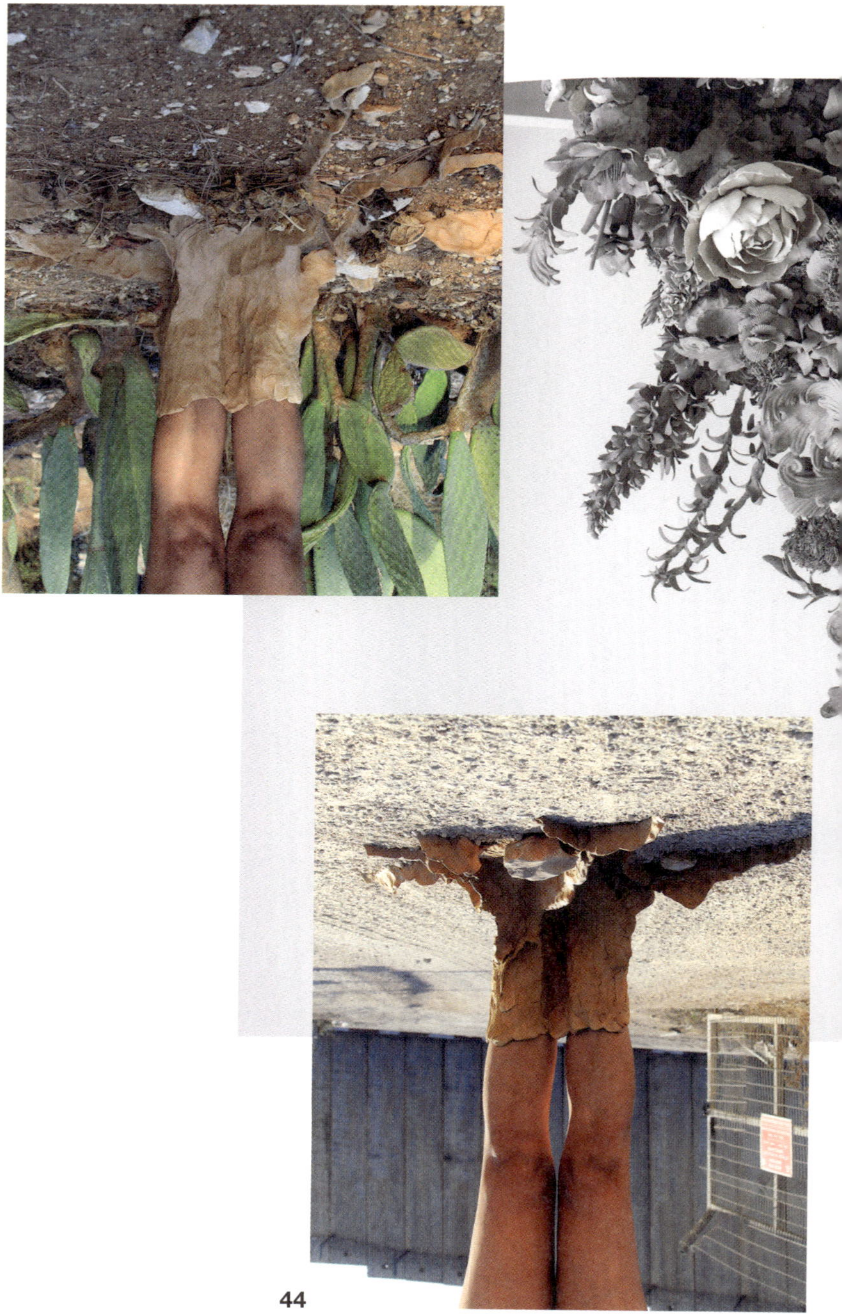

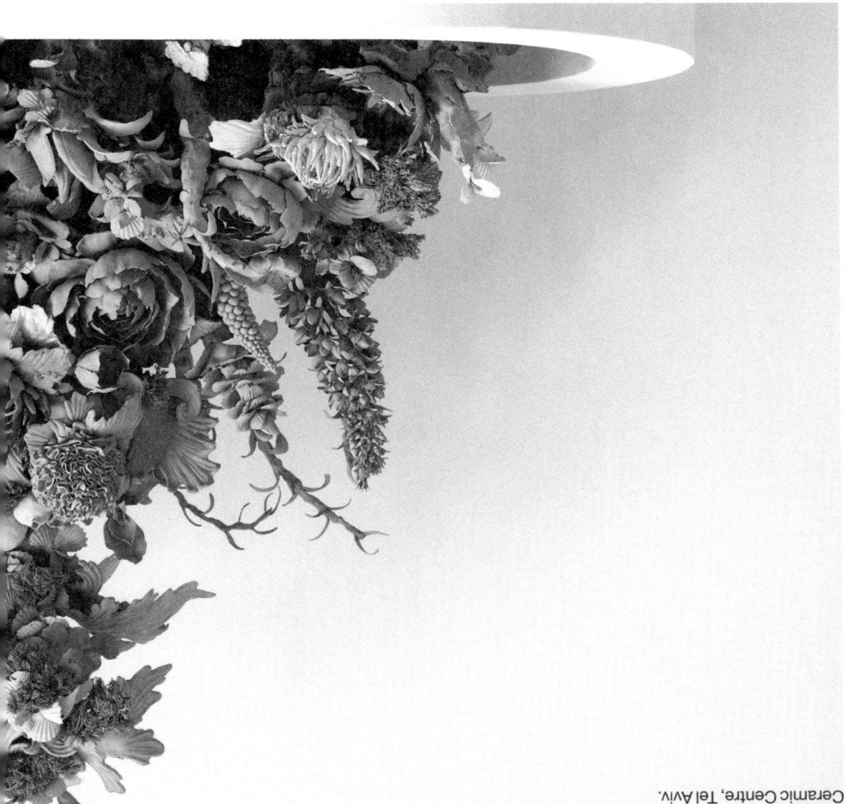

Phoebe Cummings, *Triumph of the Immaterial*, Woman's Hour Craft Prize, V&A Museum, London, 2017. Photo by Sylvain Deleu.

Opposite:

Neha Kudchadkar, *home/land*, 2016. Photos by Neha Kudchadkar/ Noa Bachner.

home/land is a series of photographs made for the "Postcolonialism?" residency and exhibition at the Benyamini Contemporary Ceramic Centre, Tel Aviv.

and industry around the world."[3] Far from a fearful Frankensteinian posthumanity, her experiments are indicative of fertile opportunities for post-craft practice, embracing the interdisciplinarities, technologies, and materials of our time.

Unhoming

Such decodings have triggered revised interpretations of home and gendered space. A string of redefinitions of domestic space – notably by men – has also removed the conventional association of craft with a female habitat and feminized practices. The Italian duo Formafantasma, Andrea Trimarchi and Simone Farresin, led the way in rethinking the nature of domestic products. There is also a recognition of displacement, homelessness, and migration whereby home is a fixed memory or fantasy. Doh Ho Suh's sewn fabric replicas of places he once lived in or Thomas Demand's modeled environments made of paper and card are based on meticulous processes and material manipulation that consume time and incise memory through scissor cuts and joins.

Roger Hiorns's Artangel project *Seizure* (2008/13) was a landmark in material alteration and emotional affect, whereby copper-sulphate crystals slowly encrusted an entire abandoned ground-floor apartment in London, a literal growth of form which nevertheless contained its own decay – a recapitulation of the fusion of liveliness and deathliness in the character of post-craft. A key feature of all these projects is a human ambivalence about home. With the lack of space to socialize at home, young people take to the Underground to knit communally, or join embroidery and quilting groups in cafés and pubs.

In terms of objects, there are now seminal examples that highlight the "unhomely," Freud's term for "everything that ought to have remained secret and hidden but has come to light."[4] This applies to the way Thomas Thwaites turned a domestic product into a discourse on craft, human values, and natural resources when in 2009 he made a toaster from scratch, sourcing all the materials and hand processing every element; the result was a dysfunctional

3/ "About," on Alexandra Daisy Ginsberg's website, accessed September 27, 2019, https://www.daisyginsberg.com/about.

4/ Sigmund Freud, "The 'Uncanny,'" in *Writings on Art and Literature* (Stanford, CA: Stanford University Press, 1997), 200.

toaster priced at £1,187.54, 250 times the cost of the toaster he had first dismantled and examined. Like all good satire, Thwaites's cycle of production and consumption exposes the unwitting significance of domestic possessions with their consumerist fetishes and tastes. Post-craft changes things and also us. Thwaites's subsequent absurdist experiment was to imitate life as a mountain goat, documented in his book *GoatMan: How I Took a Holiday from Being Human* (2016). This involved fabricating prosthetics, which enabled appropriate posture and limb movement. The project transcended hierarchical clichés of pets at home and explored the respective physicality of mammals and things.

The emphasis on things as tools reasserts the interdependence of craft and industry, one of the tenets of post-craft that salutes the continuum of making from architecture through art, craft, design, and manufacture. The maker movement, embedded in the third and fourth industrial revolutions of automation and digitization, is explored in the books of Chris Anderson and Peter Marsh, respectively *Makers: The New Industrial Revolution* (2012) and *The New Industrial Revolution: Consumers, Globalisation and the End of Mass Production* (2013). Both titles put craft know-how at the forefront of the creative industries and explain the success of the major 2011 exhibition "Power of Making," curated by Daniel Charny and organized with the Crafts Council at the V&A.

This post-craft privileging of process over product lies at the heart of expanded craft practices; today, objects and whole houses can be modeled by 3D printing. Taking this to the next step, objects can be completely superseded by in-the-moment experiences: witness Echo Morgan's digital/analogue self-presentation, Joanna Wardrop's street theater, Clare Twomey's set of manufacturing instructions sent to China by fax for her 2010–11 *Made in China* installation, or Yann Gerstberger's pressing of threads from mops onto vinyl to create tapestries, inspired by the French artist's move to Mexico in 2012, which elide two and three dimensions to "propose craftsmanship itself as an image making technique."[5]

5/ "Trudy Benson & Yann Gerstberger at Lyles & King," *Art Viewer*, July 19, 2017, https://artviewer.org/trudy-benson-yann-gerstberger-at-lyles-king/.

Self-Determining

The apparent futility of a vision of stable domestic objecthood in a place called home has found its ultimate expression in the art of Marina Abramović, a key marker of post-craft practice focused on phenomenology and the body as subject/object. In many of her performances, Abramović places herself at the mercy of an audience in a white-cube gallery and, using her body as an active instrument, triggers an audience experience and her own metamorphosis. Rather than the gendering of person, place, and things in a sphere called home, Abramović creates a testimony to her own executive power in the gallery space. The emphasis is on auto-ethnography and collective participation by visitors as witnesses, even codependents in participatory action and reaction.

It is the ultimate DIY, another feature of post-craft. We now accept the amateur as auteur in post-craft, questioning the authority of experts – a revision of the concept of give-and-take relating to production and consumption. Making (by) oneself and self-making can be equated to self-fashioning. Underlying this approach and its aesthetics are an ethics of production. The clothes design and making of Ma Ke in China is an exemplar of post-craft resistance to classification, with her shaman-like clothes that use encrusted painted raw sheeting and old tarpaulins. Her brand, Wuyong (Useless), examines the concept of "uselessness" and highlights the apparent ephemeral frivolity of fashion. Beyond classification and order inherent in fashion and museum collections, post-craft questions the longevity of existence of things and their criteria for collection.

Post-craft thus resists authority. Self-determining underpins recent democratizing maker economies in the West. The Etsy website has produced a globalized maker-seller site unmediated by institutions and "authorized" judgments. Craftivists create opportunities for collective making as part of radical social change toward empowerment in local communities. Disenfranchised groups have been the focus for DIY work to empower oneself and others, including Makerversity and Fixperts. Sociopolitical realities have brought groups to action, from Podemos to Occupy and Extinction Rebellion, using craft processes to create makeshift habitats, T-shirts, banners, publications, and masks, while local action in impoverished communities triggers social change.

Post-craft embraces the provisional and pragmatic quotidian products of protest alongside the conceptually speculative discourse of professionalized practice. Both facets are exemplified by the practice of Theaster Gates, who balances a white-cube gallery career with local projects in his hometown of Chicago, providing transformative opportunities to disadvantaged Black Americans. The same can be seen in Assemble, the Turner Prize–winning UK-based architecture collective, who create innovative buildings and who in 2013 set up a craft design and production workshop in Liverpool's Granby Street, an area where terraced housing was threatened with demolition and communities with eviction.

These DIY, self-fashioned, communitarian models of making raise questions about the nature of labor, what constitutes "good work" in society in an international context of, for example, zero-hours work, factory work, or subsistence farmwork, or equally of artificial intelligence and robot-driven services. This is the subject of Howard Gardner's ongoing project *Good Work* at Harvard University, and relates to Richard Sennett's books from the past two decades, including *The Corrosion on Character: The Personal Consequences of Work in the New Capitalism* (1998) and *Building and Dwelling: Ethics for the City* (2018). Grounding a better society in good work may echo the Arts and Crafts Movement, but the contemporary tools of communication and the hazards of contemporary employment raise far more complex problems regarding identities and communities globally.

Globalizing

Forms of good work have resided in cohesive communities now threatened by the economic imperatives of globalization. This suggests a literal definition of post-craft, where the survival of craft-based communities is threatened, for example, in Southeast Asian villages where locally grown raw materials and their crafting have hitherto been integrated into the culture and economic sustainability of a particular people. In those contexts, rituals and symbols are invoked to secure a sense of shared meaning. Their continuing significance is both threatened and questioned, for example, by Brian Jungen's totemic works in relation to Native communities in North America, eloquently discussed by Bill Brown in *Other Things* (2015), or by Kapka Kassabova in her book *Border: A Journey to the Edge of Europe* (2017), which considers the elaborate costumes, face decoration, and headdresses of Pamak brides in Bulgaria.

The post-craft condition cannot rely on benign cultural, economic, and sociopolitical exchange for mutual benefit. In the poignant performative series "home/land," created during a residency based in Israel in 2017, the Indian ceramicist Neha Kudchadkar marks sensitive sites in Jerusalem and the West Bank with clay molds of her feet: "I question notions of ownership and control. I suggest rootedness and uprootedness. (In order to cause distress and claim land, settlers famously uproot olive trees that have been a part of Palestinian families). I also refer to the first act of asserting right to the earth – by planting trees and crops – the means by which the human species has colonized the earth."[6] Making this recent work in contested territory carried risks of discovery: it serves as a literal placement to mark displacement, part of the psychogeographic turn in post-craft.

A catchword for the condition of post-craft is therefore "de-territorialization." Local things made with local materials for local communities have dispersed into a web of nomadism and migratory and virtual networks across the globe. This shift is manifested in post-craft works such as the gigantic ceramic and bricolage installations globally exhibited by Thai Canadian artist Linda Sormin. It is a de-territorialized condition explained by Nicolas Bourriaud's conception of the "altermodern," articulated in his exhibition at Tate Britain in 2009 and his manifesto:

Multiculturalism and identity is being overtaken by creolisation: Artists are now starting from a globalised state of culture.

6/ "home/land," on Neha Kudchakar's website, accessed July 25, 2020, http://www.nehakudchadkar.com/?portfolio=homeland.

This new universalism is based on translations, subtitling and generalised dubbing […] The artist becomes 'homo viator,' the prototype of the contemporary traveller whose passage through signs and formats refers to a contemporary experience of mobility […]. The form of the work expresses a course, a wandering, rather than a fixed space-time.[7]

Narrating

The "homo viator" is operating in what has been called a "post-truth society," one resistant to authenticity. This is why entire urban groups try to embed artisanal processes in daily life as an inscription of real time, place, material, and thing. One can propose the equation post-truth = post-institution = post-craft. Museums, organizations, and arts schools concerned with the future of craft through collection, promotion, and education are grappling with the pluralities of practices and contexts.

In searching for narratives of the post-craft condition, it is therefore appropriate that fictions and counterfactuals are included. To name just some of the practitioners in this dense activity: the fantasy scenarios of power relations in Naomi Alderman's *The Power* (2016), Tom McCarthy's *Satin Island* (2015), and Charlie Brooker's TV series *Black Mirror*, first aired in 2011; the biographies of things, people, and places epitomized by W. G. Sebald and Orhan Pamuk; Adam Curtis's sociopolitical 2016 documentary *HyperNormalisation*; and research on place by Forensic Architecture. Industrialization, feminism, and postcolonialism – progressive positives in modernity – give tangible legacies grounded in unequal economies and politics, as theorist Mark Fisher explained more than a decade ago in *Capitalist Realism: Is There No Alternative?* (2009). Today it is not the alternative but a later phase being played out in a postindustrial, digital, synthetic, data-driven universe. The post-craft universe.

Craft is broad in theory and practice. As with postmodernism – a set of features in cultural production extrapolated from modernism – post-craft marks out a continuously shape-shifting field. Ultimately, post-craft describes an era of practices that help us consider the ever-shifting shape of things in our lives.

7/ Nicolas Bourriaud, "Altermodern Explained: Manifesto," Tate Modern, 2009, https://www.tate.org.uk/whats-on/tate-britain/exhibition/altermodern/altermodern-explain-altermodern/altermodern-explained.

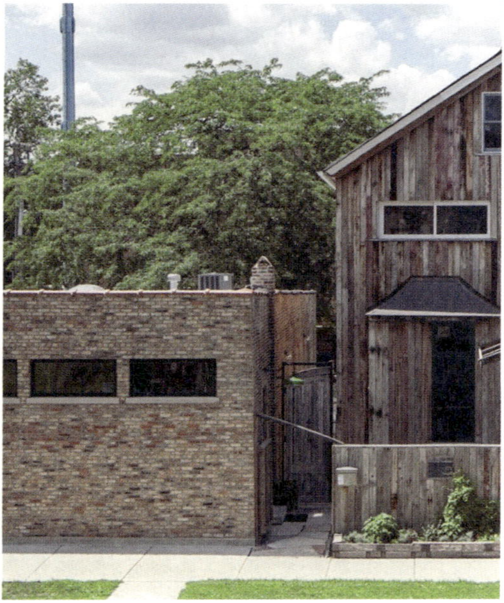

Theaster Gates/Rebuild Foundation, *The Archive House*, Chicago, 2010.

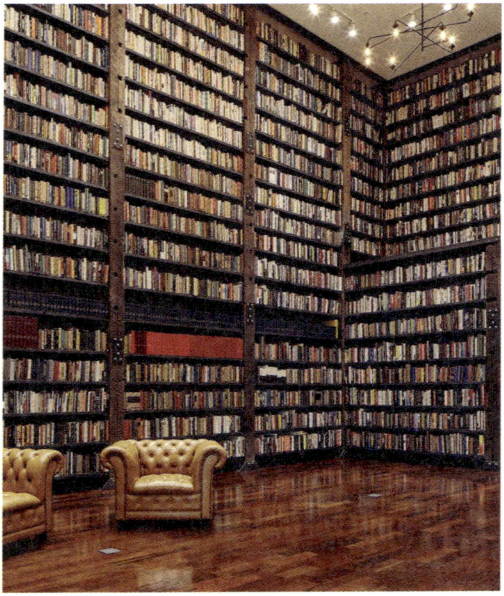

Theaster Gates/Rebuild Foundation, *Stony Island Arts Bank*, Chicago, 2015. Photo by Tom Harris.

MADE IN
MADE IN
CHINA/
CHINA/
CHINA/
CHINA/
CREATED IN
CREATED IN
CHINA

CATHARINE
ROSSI

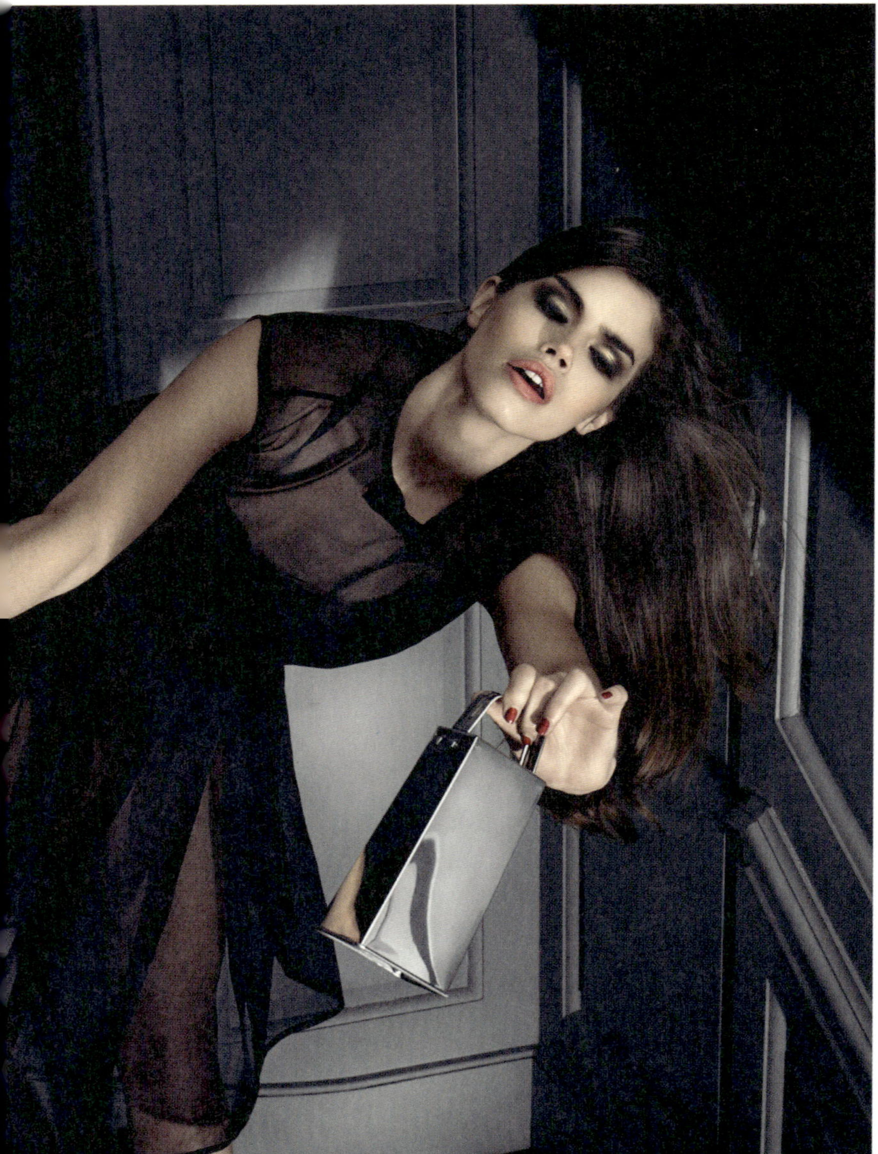

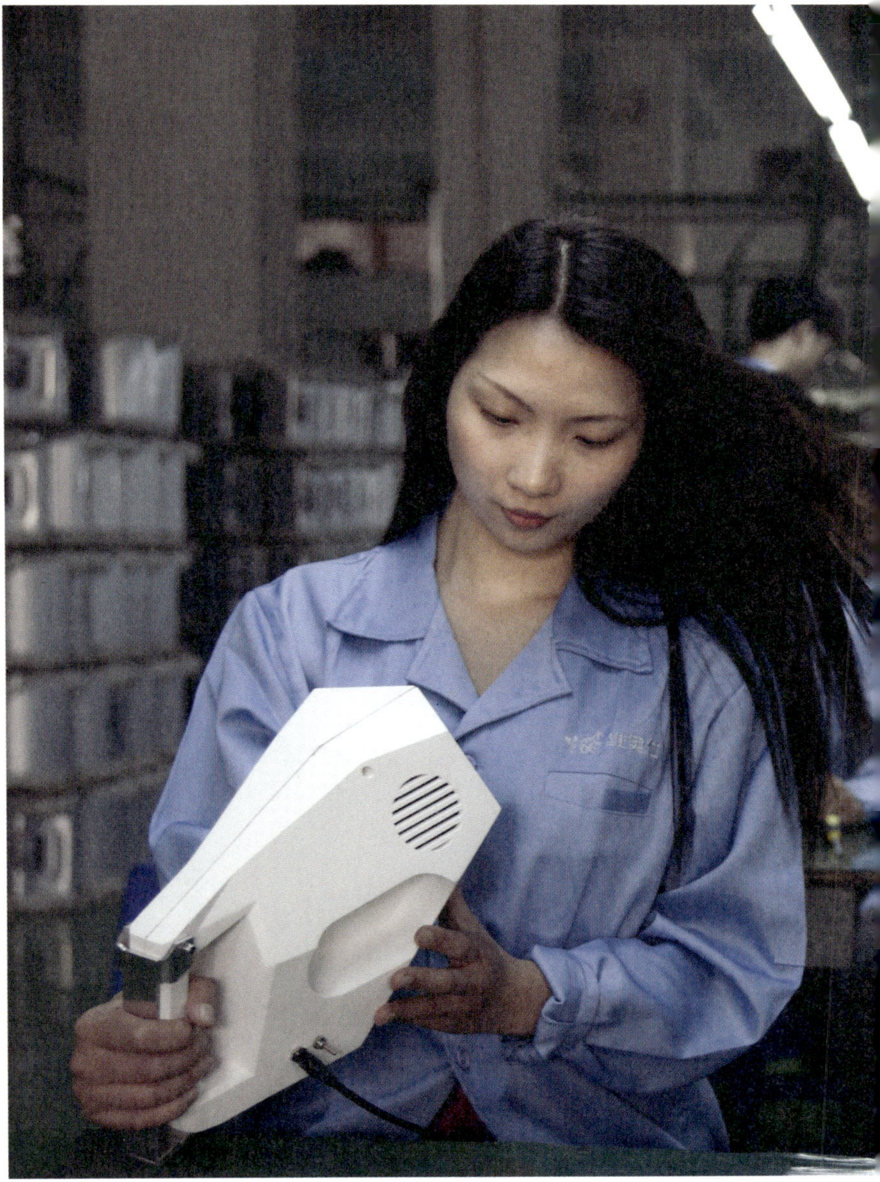

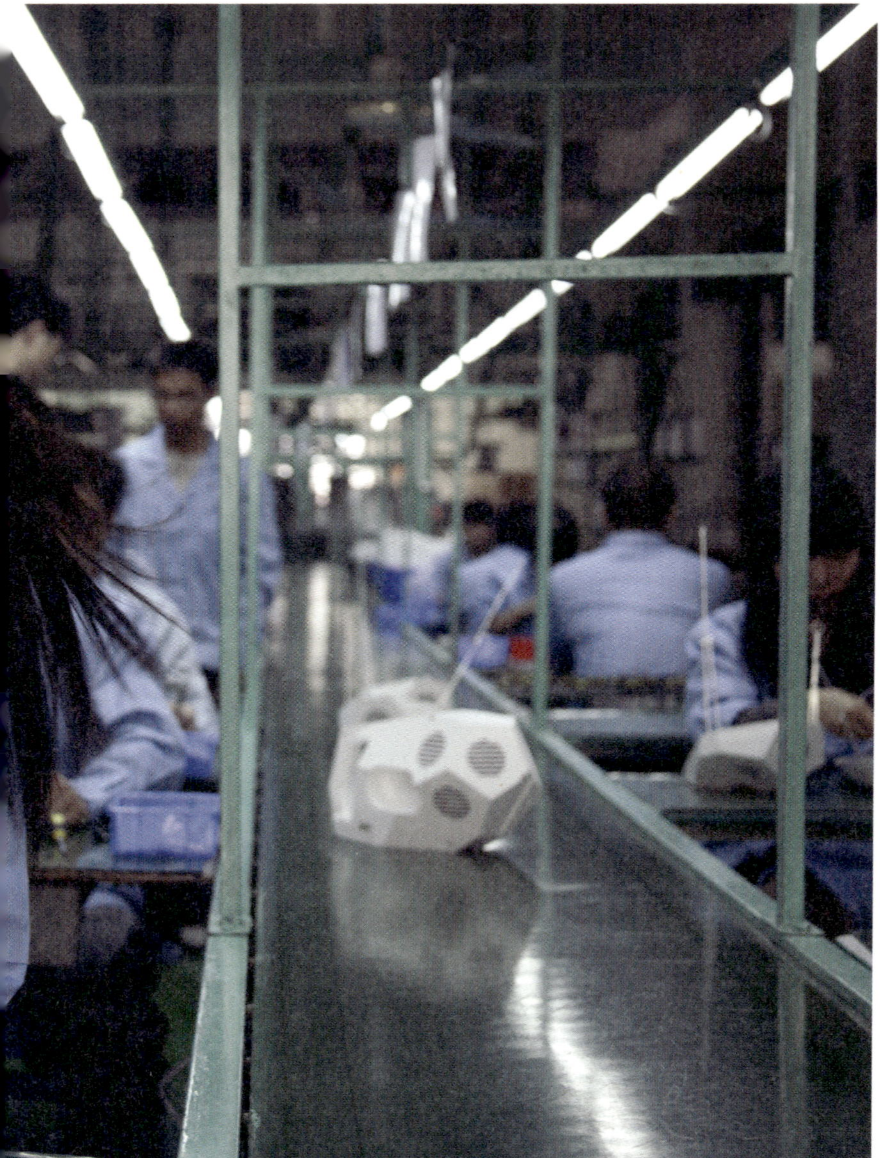

Made in China / Created in China

Catharine Rossi

A camera pans along a production line in a factory located in Zhongshan, a city in the Pearl River Delta, southeastern China. It tracks the assembly of an electronic product along a green conveyor belt as it is transformed from a half shell of plastic casing into a completed white good. Positioned along the belt are young Chinese men and women in identikit blue jackets, their repetitive movements caught on camera as they twist and cut wires, affix antennae, construct and test the finished product. In the background, stacks of completed goods and more assembly lines are visible; a noisy industrial setting that furnishes the film's soundtrack.

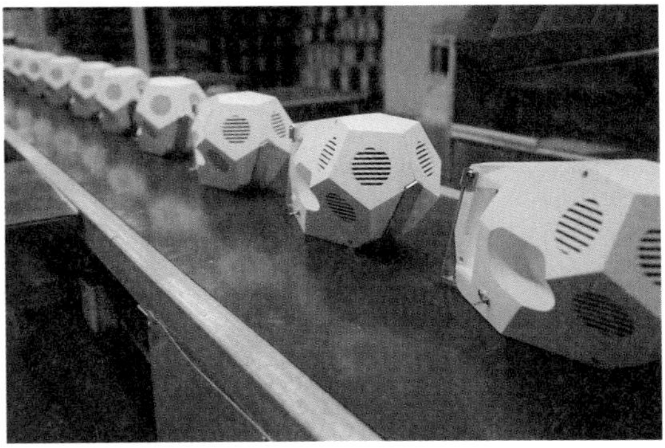

Page 54:

Jeremy Hutchison, advertisement for *Erratum®*, 2012, a dysfunctional object designed and manufactured by factory worker Zeng Wei Cheng, Yangjiang Dreamhome Industrial Co. Ltd, Yangjiang. Photo by Charlotte Kibbles.

Pages 55–57:

Revital Cohen & Tuur Van Balen, film stills from *75 Watt*, 2013.

Conceived by London-based artist duo Revital Cohen & Tuur Van Balen in 2013, *75 Watt* is reminiscent of a well-known film of China's production line: *Manufactured Landscapes*, Jennifer Baichwal's 2006 documentary of fellow Canadian Edward Burtynsky, a photographer who captures the industrializing transformations of the global environment. Baichwal's film opens with a transfixing eight-minute tracking shot of a huge factory in Zhangzhou, also in the Pearl River Delta, in which seemingly never-ending rows of workers manually assemble electronic irons. Both Burtynsky's documentary and photographs of the factory make manifest the near-inhuman nature of China's factories, as they feed a seemingly insatiable global need for electronic goods.

Despite their visual similarities, the key difference between *75 Watt* and *Manufactured Landscapes* is that the former is a fictional film. Although it is set in a real factory, the cast is a mix of factory employees and volunteers who put together a nonfunctional product designed solely by how the assembly line orchestrates their bodily movements. Motivated by an interest in the biopolitics of the globalized mass manufacturing economy and how this conditions the worker's body, Cohen and Van Balen created a multimedia project that put the act of making at its fore.[1] The artists worked with the English choreographer Alexander Whitley to create a performance that comments on and exposes the place of people in production systems that often appear abstract, anonymous, and automated.

1/ See "75 Watt," on Revital Cohen & Tuur Van Balen's website, http://www.cohenvanbalen.com/work/75-watt#.

75 Watt was informed by the labor conditions of the majority of China's production lines in the early 2010s. It came in the wake of a spate of worker suicides in the delta, whose factories constitute the epicenter of global electronics manufacturing. The artists cite a survey produced by the American NGO China Labor Watch, who recorded 76 suicides between 2000 and 2010. In 2012 around 150 workers threatened to jump off the roof of Foxconn, the electronics giant responsible for manufacturing Apple products, as a protest against the working conditions in its factories.[2]

2/ Oli Stratford and Lori Gibbs, "75 Watt in the Pearl River Delta," *Disegno Daily*, February 20, 2014, https://www.disegnodaily.com/article/75-watt-in-the-pearl-river-delta.

Such dismal news stories only affirm the negative view of "Made in China," a manufacturing ecology seen as synonymous with the exploitative and environmentally damaging globalized economy of the late twentieth and early twenty-first centuries, one built on the outsourcing of production to ever cheaper economies embroiled in the manufacture of products that reveal little about their often dubious origins.

Concern about this situation is in part what has fueled the ongoing craft resurgence that emerged in the mid-2000s. Following the 2007–8 global financial crisis, many have looked to the handmade for its seemingly more ethical and environmental associations. This includes a small set of Western artists and designers who chose to directly comment on the culture of Chinese manufacturing by creating products and production scenarios that are not just made in China, but are about Made in China, using making to address issues from copying to craftsmanship, agency, and the environmental impact of mass production.

Copying as Craftsmanship

Since China first opened up to trade in 1978, Western firms and manufacturers have been attracted to it as a place to outsource production and open factories.[3] This has contributed to China's growth as an economic superpower, which saw it take over from the United States as the world's largest manufacturer in 2010, contributing to the decline of manufacturing in the West.[4] As such a threat, it is no wonder that China has been considered a site of low-skilled labor and poor production quality, capable of only producing cheap copies rather than creative innovation.

While intellectual property theft has played a significant part in China's growth, the reality is more complex. This is partly due to the cultural specificity of copying in China, which is both different from and more varied than in the West. Alongside copies whose difference to the original is palpable (*fangzhipin*) sit exact reproductions

3/ See Tim Lindgren, "Chinese Fashion Designers: Rebuilding from the Centre of the World," *Handbook of Cultural and Creative Industries in China*, ed. Michael Keane (Cheltenham, UK; Elgar, 2016), 471; and Neil Ewins, *Ceramics and Globalization: Staffordshire Ceramics, Made in China* (London: Bloomsbury, 2017), 53–56.

4/ Peter Marsh, "China Noses Ahead as Top Goods Producer," *Financial Times*, March 13, 2011, https://www.ft.com/content/002fd8f0-4d96-11e0-85e4-00144feab49a.

(*fuzhipin*) whose verisimilitude accords them the same status as the originals on which they are based.[5] The Dutch designer Maarten Baas, whose work oscillates between gallery and production-focused works, explored this concept in *Plastic Chair in Wood* (2008), the result of a commission by Shanghai's Contrast Gallery to explore creative techniques in China. Baas worked with the city's woodworkers and tasked them with reimagining existing furniture in carved elm wood, a specialization in the area. The most notable of these was his challenge to make an exact re-creation of the plastic monobloc chair. The mid-century stackable design is the world's most mass-produced chair, injection-molded from a single piece of plastic and manufactured at huge scales in China and elsewhere.[6]

5/ Byung-Chul Han, *Shanzhai: Deconstruction in Chinese* (Cambridge, MA: MIT Press, 2017), 60.

6/ Brendan Cormier, *Values of Design* (London: Victoria & Albert, 2017), 75.

Produced in a limited edition of fifty, the local artisans used Chinese joinery techniques to slot and glue together the individual pieces of the chair in a slow, labor-intensive, and highly specialized production process that respected the specificity of their copying material, demonstrating an understanding of materiality that is central to craftsmanship. The resulting hand-carved chair bore an uncanny likeness to the plastic original in all but material and color. For Baas this similarity was intentional, as it revealed the contradictory complexity of Made in China: "To me, 'made in China' has a double connotation: it stands for cheap, plastic mass products and, at the same time, labour intensive traditional fine craftsmanship, like Chinese calligraphy, paintings, porcelains and intricate carvings. Moreover, China is known for making copies of original works. By copying a typical cheap, plastic mass product like the famous monobloc chair into a labour-intensive hand carved object, I tried to capture all these characteristics in one chair."[7]

7/ "Plastic Chair in Wood," on Maarten Baas's website, 2008, http://maartenbaas.com/plastic-chair-in-wood/.

Baas isn't the only practitioner to use imitation to highlight skilled craftsmanship in China, and to use such a well-known mass-manufactured product to do so. In 2006 the American artist Sam Durant approached the Jiao Zhi studio, a porcelain factory in Xiamen on the southeast coast of China. Durant, whose work is characterized by its engagement with social, cultural, and political issues, commissioned nine porcelain copies of the monobloc chair, and tasked the factory's workers to produce a series of chairs freehand rather than using a mold.[8] Each of the chairs, glazed in a different bright color, is willfully unique with different patterns on its seat back. Here the visibly individual, one-off associations of the handmade are highlighted, a feature emphasized by the naming of the chairs: each chair has its own title, which includes the names of all the workers involved in its making and the name of the factory.

8/ Glenn Adamson and Julia Bryan-Wilson, *Art in the Making: Artists and Their Materials from the Studio to Crowdsourcing* (London: Thames & Hudson, 2016), 226.

Like Baas's *Plastic Chair in Wood*, Durant's decision to have this cheap, ubiquitous chair skillfully crafted as a one-off in a precious material, and to credit the individuals who made it, was intended to oppose the derogative connotations of Made in China and the cheap copying with which it is synonymous. It was also conceived as a form of postcolonial critique. In his description of the project, Durant cites the West's role in creating the concept of Made in China. For him the monobloc chair is "indicative of globalization and the spread of western (Euro-American), post nationalist capitalism. Manufacturing of the resin chairs can be easily accomplished in the country with the cheapest labor and/or most advantageous business climate and then shipped for sale anywhere. This system [is] geared toward maximum profit, usually through maximum exploitation."[9]

9/ "Porcelain Chairs," on Sam Durant's website, 2012, http://samdurant.net/index.php/project/porcelain-chairs/.

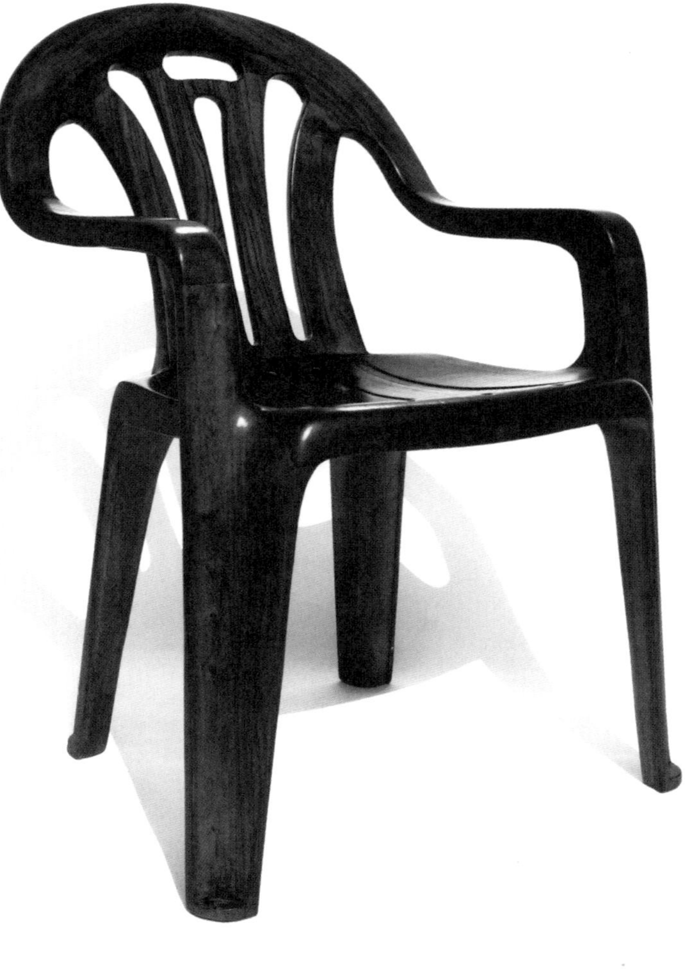

Studio Maarten Baas, *Plastic Chair in Wood*, 2008. Courtesy of Pearl Lam Galleries, Shanghai.

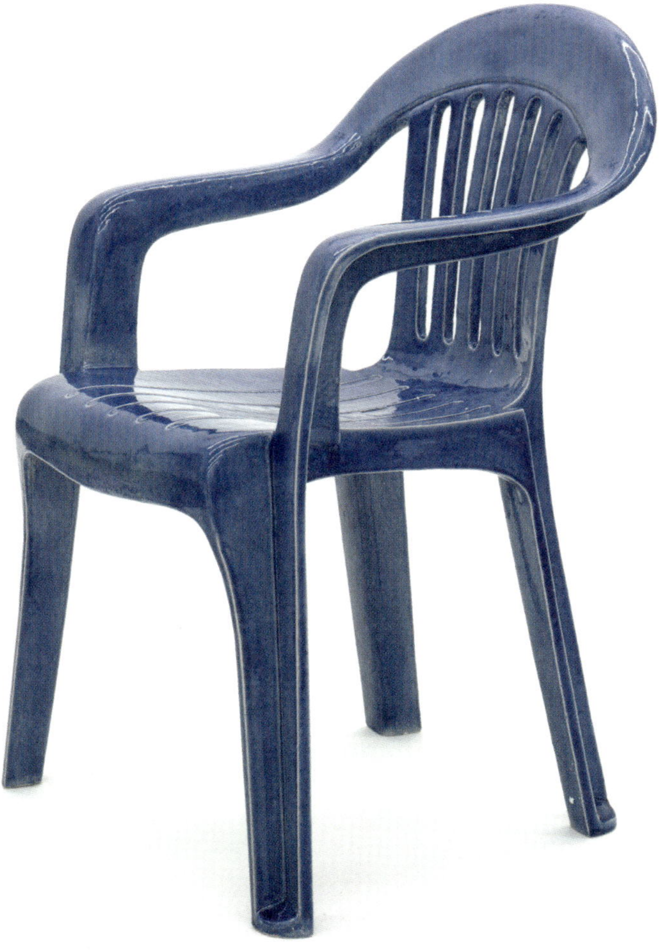

Sam Durant, *Blue*, unique monobloc resin chair, 2006. Photo by Joshua White.

As a Western artist commissioning work from Chinese makers, Durant is also part of the very exploitative system he critiques, something he recognizes.[10] The problem of the privileged Western artist and the power imbalance between artist and maker informs all the works discussed here. Durant is at least aware of this issue, even if he is unable to solve it.

10/ See "Porcelain Chairs."

Giving Agency through Making

Numerous artists have attempted to address this inequality by creating projects in which Chinese makers are accorded a greater role in the production process, engendering an agency associated with craft's ethical credentials. In 2012 the artist Jeremy Hutchison sent emails to a number of factories, in which he requested that one of its workers make a mistake in the production of a mass-produced good. Other than the requirement to render the product dysfunctional, the workers were given complete freedom to make any errors they wished. *Erratum* is characteristic of Hutchison's interest in intervening in production systems, often with political aims. For this project, he engaged with factories all over the world, although notably *Erratum* was informed in particular by Chinese manufacturing, specifically the allegations about the working conditions in Foxconn that also troubled Cohen and Van Balen. Hutchison cites a worker who described how "sometimes he would deliberately drop something on the ground so that he could have a few seconds of rest while picking it up." In response, Hutchinson also sought to change the worker's bodily experience of the production line: he saw the deliberate introduction of a mistake, what he describes as normally the "exhausted worker's gesture," as a means to introduce a moment of rest and freedom into the relentless assembly line.[11] While making mistakes

11/ "Erratum®," on Jeremy Hutchison's website, 2012, http://www.jeremyhutchison.com/work/project47.html.

has no place in mass manufacture, it does in craft: the nineteenth-century art historian John Ruskin said that the freedom to make mistakes was the mark of the human presence in production.

Like *75 Watt*, *Erratum* consists of one-off products that uncannily combine the familiar and the dysfunctional, including a cheese grater without holes, a ladder with different-length legs, and a golf club with a twisted handle. Notably, both projects are also reliant on design and production decisions that occur through an international exchange of emails, a detached and distant communication process that inevitably raised confusion, particularly given Hutchinson's unusual invitation. The manufacturers could not understand the nature of a request that opposed the quest for anonymous perfection, which is at the heart of global mass manufacture.[12]

12/ See "Erratum®."

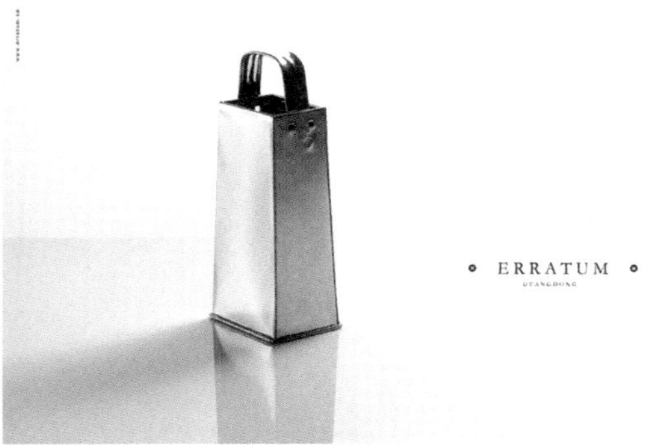

Jeremy Hutchison, advertisement for *Erratum®*, 2012, a dysfunctional object designed and manufactured by factory worker Zeng Wei Cheng, Yangjiang Dreamhome Industrial Co. Ltd, Yangjiang. Photo by Jonathan Minster.

In 2014, Cohen and Van Balen explored both the idea of giving agency to makers and the language of international outsourcing in *Giving More to Gain More*, a series of large-scale aluminum structures embedded with programmable LED strips. The works display fragments of correspondence between the artists and the Chinese LED manufacturers for

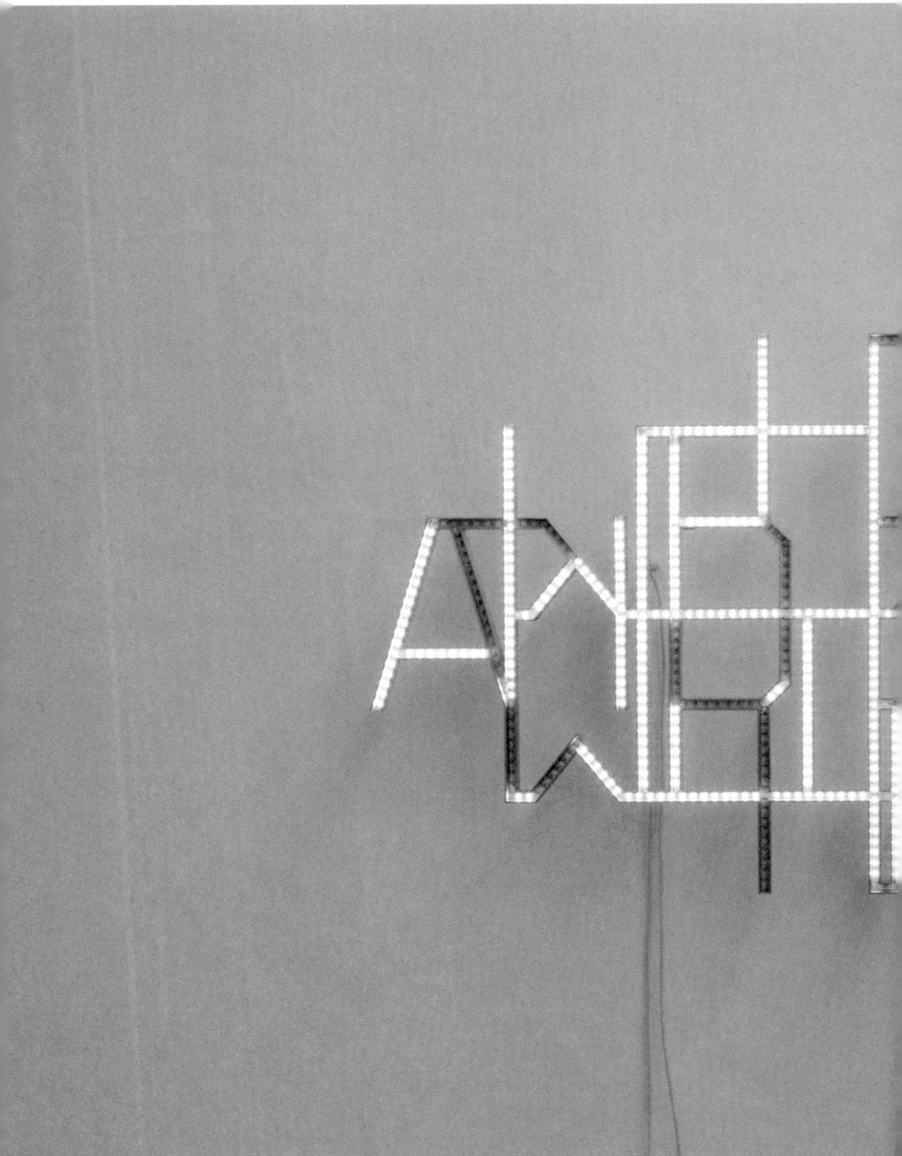

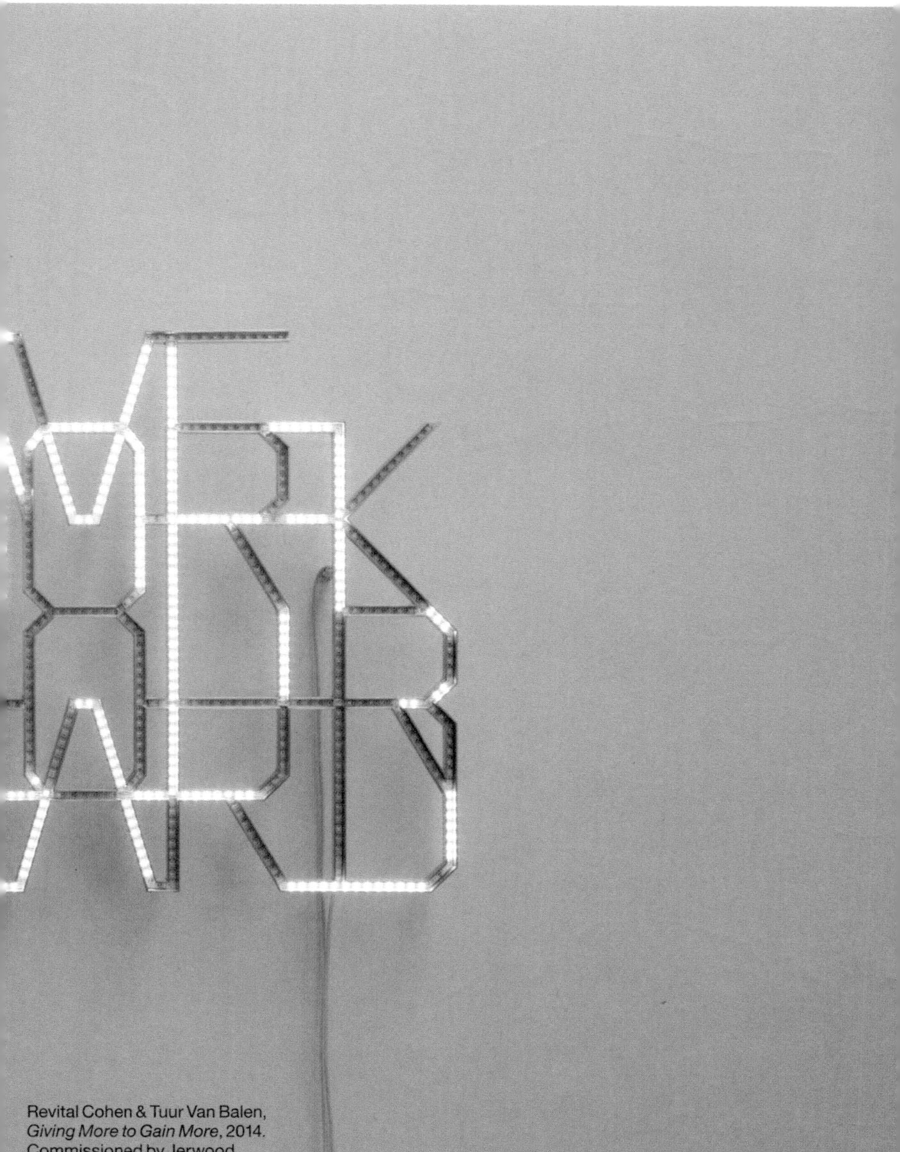

Revital Cohen & Tuur Van Balen, *Giving More to Gain More*, 2014. Commissioned by Jerwood Visual Art.

75 Watt and *Nowhere a Shadow*, an installation commissioned for the 2014 Lisbon Architecture Biennale. The language that emerged from this digital exchange sparked an interest in what the artists term a "production-centred pidgin poetry."[13] They selected the phrases of one of the individuals they had contact with – April – and scaled them up to appear on the structures: "We Have to Work Hard and Work with Our Heart," "Customers Are Real People and Real Feeling," and "It Is So Brightness." Echoing Durant, Cohen and Van Balen explain that they wanted to give April a voice. While the project does this, it is also difficult to overcome the near-comedic quality of the inaccurate "pidgin" English that potentially further denigrates, rather than celebrates, this Chinese maker.

13/ "Giving More to Gain More," on Revital Cohen & Tuur Van Balen's website, http://www.cohenvanbalen.com/work/giving-more-to-gain-more#.

What is effective is the contrast between April's heartfelt, human expressions and the cold, impersonal nature of the metal structure; a reminder of the humans who are ultimately present in all industrial manufacture. This presence features in another way in *Giving More to Gain More*. The work was the result of a commission for the Jerwood Makers Open 2014, a biennial competition for UK-based practitioners launched in 2010 to champion both "makers and making."[14] Accordingly, while the words and LED lighting came from China, the artists made the aluminum structures in the United Kingdom, welding and soldering the lighting tracks themselves, deliberately reversing the directionality of East-West production relations.[15] Looking more like the product of a machine than a hand, they are reminders that craft can take multiple guises.

14/ "Jerwood Makers Open," Jerwood Arts, accessed June 14, 2019, https://jerwoodarts.org/exhibitionsandevents/opportunities/jerwood-makers-open/.

15/ Basia Lewandowska Cummings, "Conversations with April," Jerwood Arts, 2014, https://jerwoodarts.org/exhibitionsandevents/writing-and-media/conversations-with-april/.

Making Material Environmentalism

While craft became a major cultural force in the 2000s, industrial manufacturing still dominates the global landscape. One of the most striking, and disturbing, aspects of Edward Burtynsky's photography is the undeniable impact of mass manufacture on the natural landscape. In 2014, the London-based Unknown Fields Division focused on this problem, specifically on the impact of the Chinese production of everyday electronic goods. Directed by Liam Young and Kate Davies, the nomadic design studio investigated the rare-earth metals that are found in everything from batteries to camera lenses and magnets. The environmental consequences of this mining industry are vast. According to the V&A Museum, "one tonne of rare earth produces 75 tonnes of acidic waste water, a cocktail of acids, heavy metals, carcinogens and radioactive material at three times background radiation."[16] The collective combined film and making to make their point. Working with the ceramist Kevin Callaghan, they used the mud from a toxic lake and dump near a rare-earth mine in Inner Mongolia to make three ceramic vessels. Echoing Ming-dynasty porcelain vases, the sizes of each are indexical of the amount of toxic waste that results from the production of three electronic commodities – a smartphone, laptop, and electric car battery cell.[17] The results are appropriately abject funereal urns that are epitaphs to the waste caused by consumers in countries often far removed from sites of production. Made in the United Kingdom, these vessels are criticisms of global capitalism and its effects aimed at the West as well as the East, making clear that we are all complicit in "Made in China."

While China has been the "factory of the world" for nearly a half century, the profits of its exploits do not reside primarily there but instead with the largely Western companies and countries where goods are often designed. As Brendan Cormier in the United States, the V&A's lead curator of the museum's outpost in Shenzhen described, "for every iPhone produced in Shenzhen, China's profit

16/ "Rare Earthenware," V&A Museum, December 8, 2015, http://collections.vam.ac.uk/item/O1326005/rare-earthenware-vessel-unknown-fields-division/.

17/ "Rare Earthenware: Radioactive Ceramics Commission for the Victoria and Albert Museum," *Unknown Fields Division*, 2014, http://www.unknownfieldsdivision.com/summer2014china-aworldadriftpart02.html.

(primarily through labor costs) is roughly only $10 while the vast majority (between $299 and $275) goes to Apple back in the United States."[18] This asymmetry is a persistent presence in the Western-conceived projects described here, but it also appears in Ai Weiwei's *Sunflower Seeds*, the dissident Chinese artist's 2010 commission for Tate Modern's Turbine Hall.

18/ Cormier, *Values of Design*, 17.

Referencing a Chinese tradition for large-scale works, *Sunflower Seeds* consisted of over one hundred million porcelain seeds that took up over one thousand square meters of the gargantuan Turbine Hall.[19] The huge scale of the artwork and the identikit appearance of the seeds bely the crafted nature of their production: each was individually sculpted and painted by specialist craftspeople in Jingdezhen, the southern Chinese city long renowned for ceramics production. Building on Ai's long engagement with ceramics, *Sunflower Seeds* contains multiple meanings. These include Communist Party symbolism (sunflower seeds appeared regularly in paintings of Chairman Mao), commentary on the Made in China phenomenon and its effect on China, and the place of the individual within China's mass society.[20] It is also a reminder of the people involved in making processes; the gargantuan scale of the undertaking and the human endeavor required jolts us into remembering the human presence in all production.

19/ Juliet Bingham, "Introduction," in *Ai Weiwei: Sunflower Seeds*, ed. Juliet Bingham (London: Tate Publishing, 2010), 23–24.

20/ "About the Exhibition," Tate Modern, 2010, https://www.tate.org.uk/whats-on/tate-modern/exhibition/unilever-series/unilever-series-ai-weiwei-sunflower-seeds.

Sunflower Seeds also raises issues around the different expectations for makers in different parts of the world, and the inequality between artist, audience, and maker. Initially, visitors were invited to walk across the installation and feel the porcelain crumble underfoot. Shortly after it opened, this was prohibited because of concerns over the potentially damaging effects of inhaling porcelain dust. Visitors were therefore allowed only to see the sunflower landscape from a distance. While this decision rightly protected the audience, as Glenn Adamson and Julia Bryan-Wilson have pointed out, such protection was not afforded to the workers who spent two years making the seeds, inhaling this potentially dangerous dust for a sustained period. "That Tate had a clear duty of care to one of those groups, and not the other, exemplified all too clearly the uncomfortable realities of global production systems: the very topic that the project had meant to address, albeit not so directly."[21] *Sunflower Seeds* therefore unwittingly unravels any romanticism around craft making – the production of the seeds was a repetitive and potentially harmful undertaking – but it also asserts the inequality of the politics of production that appears throughout the projects discussed here.

21/ Adamson and Bryan-Wilson, *Art in the Making*, 173.

While these are not the only practitioners to have engaged with the concept of Made in China, they represent both the approaches and the themes that characterized this small trend. Notably, all these projects arose between 2010 and 2014. While designers and artists have continued to have their work produced in China, the interest in making work that comments on Made in China seems to have ebbed. This could be because the productive reality this phrase denotes has itself changed. Since 2004 the Chinese government has been championing a shift from Made in China to "Created in China," a strategy intended to move the country up the value supply chain toward a knowledge-based, value-added economy in which production is increasingly automated; a shift that removes people from the production line, but also unsettles the balance of power between China and the countries it does business with.[22] There has also been a shift in designers' and artists' creative practice: rather than critically

22/ Guy Julier, *Economies of Design* (London: Sage, 2017), 129.

commenting on problematic making elsewhere, many practitioners are taking direct action and seeking to make more locally, or opting to focus on other issues and strategies that may even take them away from making.

Together, these Made in China projects act as case studies for post-craft in the early twenty-first century. They demonstrate how craft has retained a role for critique that was present in the earlier craft revivals of the late-nineteenth and twentieth centuries, even as it has assumed and maintained a more mainstream status than it had historically been accorded. It demonstrates how making can still be used to raise craft-associated questions such as the presence of agency, skill, and ethics in production. The short-lived nature of these projects, which saw craft temporarily picked up by practitioners and then put down again as their gaze shifted to other questions and approaches, was inevitably the fate for any cultural phenomenon that finds itself temporarily fashionable. Whether craft can retain its critical currency at a moment when it is unclear whether it will maintain its mainstream visibility, or once again ebb into the background, is yet to be seen.

PETER DORMER SELECTIONS

INTRO– DUCED INTRO– DUCED BY BY

TANYA HARROD

Tanya Harrod

Introduction to Peter Dormer Selections

Peter Dormer (1949–1996) was a combative writer on the visual arts and architecture who thought deeply about the crafts during the 1980s and 1990s. Shaped by the cultural and political vicissitudes of postwar Britain, why do Dormer's ideas appear worth revisiting today?[1]

1/ For an autobiographical essay by Dormer, see "New Jerusalem and the Domestic Landscape," in *Our Domestic Landscape: Your Home, Whose Choice?* (Manchester: Cornerhouse, 1987), 6–14.

Dormer spent two years at art school – a foundation course at Bath Academy of Art, Corsham (1967–68), a year studying painting at Manchester College of Art (1968–69) – and then read philosophy at Bristol University (1969–72). In addition to working both as a teacher and in local government, Dormer also served as a Labour councillor in Ealing from 1978 to 1982, where he learned some tough debating skills. In 1978 he began to write for *Art Monthly*, then under the inspired editorship of Peter Townsend. In the early 1980s, Dormer made the bold decision to become a full-time writer, contributing a regular "Artlobby" column to *Art Monthly* magazine that cast a witty, disenchanted eye over state funding for the arts, fashionable theoretical writing, and the uneasy relationship between craft, design, and architecture.

Dormer's experience of art school left him with an active dislike of the institutionalized avant-garde, a prejudice he shared with Peter Fuller (1947–1990), a leading art critic of the late 1970s and 1980s who also died relatively young, aged forty-three. Both men disliked the new art practices that characterized the late 1960s and 1970s and the resulting abandonment of a range of craft skills within the fine arts. They deplored the demise of life drawing in art colleges that elevated the tools of language, photography, and film over more traditional art making. The passion of Dormer's and Fuller's writing was matched by the output of a cohort of young architecture critics who argued for a rejection of heroic and international modernism's grand narratives in favor of vernacular, regional, and historicist inspirations. This generalized call to order in art and architecture, coming at the same time as a radical Conservative government led by Margaret Thatcher, explains why Dormer and Fuller turned to the craft world for specific values. They anticipated finding a counter-discourse centered on skill, vernacular values, and a respect for everyday functionality – perhaps forgetting that younger makers had trained in the very same art colleges that had recast the practices of painting and sculpture. As a result, Fuller found that "the crafts increasingly appeal to the debased Fine Arts in order, quite literally, to validate themselves,"[2] while Dormer identified and deplored "crafts' flirtation with art."[3] Fuller penned his first article in *Crafts* magazine (the UK Crafts Council's official journal) in 1981. Dormer began to write critically in 1982 after a year as the reviews editor at *Crafts*.

2/ Peter Fuller, review of "Textiles North" (1981), in *The Naked Artist* (London: Writers & Readers, 1983), 212.

3/ Peter Dormer, "Artlobby: The Future of the Craftsman, Part 2," *Art Monthly*, no. 71, December/January 1983/84, 38.

The meaning of skill and the purpose of the crafts were two themes that dominated Dormer's writings in the 1980s and into the 1990s. He was at pains to emphasize what he believed to be the proper nature of the studio craft project: "A world of modest ideas with a straightforward vocabulary of familiar and functional forms."[4] A trio of touring shows he organized for the Crafts Council in 1983, "A Closer Look at Rugs," "Lettering," and "Wood," suggested the strengths of his approach. Each show placed the work of individuals in a social context. Lettering was discussed in conjunction with architecture, while rugs, furniture, and wood were viewed in terms of technique, design, and batch production. The processes of designing and making were explored through examples of works in progress and through diagrams and extended didactic exhibition panels.

4/ Peter Dormer, "The Ideal World of Vermeer's Little Lacemaker," in *Design after Modernism: Beyond the Object*, ed. John Thackaray (London: Thames & Hudson, 1988), 142.

In certain contexts, Dormer argued that studio craft was a peripheral activity to be contrasted with the essential and valuable work of the designer. He wrote sympathetically of the designer Jasper Morrison's repudiation of handcraft and of Morrison's discomfort with "the creamy excess of middle-class craftspeople who have retreated from production and whose existence is a luxury."[5] *The Meanings of Modern Design* (1990) took an original look at the complex relations designers have with consumers and at the symbolism and morality of product styling. This was surely the only design survey to include a disturbing photograph of an animal restrained for product testing – as an example of what cat-loving Dormer called "invisible" or "below the line" design processes kept hidden from consumers. Dormer's *The Art of the Maker* (1994), however, validated craft, much inspired by the philosopher-scientist Michael Polanyi's ideas about tacit or personal knowledge. *The Art of the Maker* was an experiential book in which Dormer grappled step-by-step with the skills of figurative clay modeling and calligraphy in an attempt to understand and bring value to the special kinds of knowledge involved in craft processes.

5/ Peter Dormer, "Utilistic Optimism," in *Jasper Morrison: Designs, Projects and Drawings, 1981–1989* (London: Architecture Design and Technology Press, 1990), 8.

All of Dormer's writing, published in magazines such as *Art Monthly* and *Marxism Today*, bristled with awkward questions and unexpected perspectives. He condemned the complacent nature of British culture, at times with a loathing that recalled Jim Dixon's tirade in *Lucky Jim*, a novel by Kingsley Amis. But he also liked to defend what he called "middle brow, middle taste" England.[6] He spoke up for skills neglected by high culture such as flower arranging, cooking, juggling, surgery, dentistry, and DIY. In Dormer's view, contemporary artists and craftspeople were less competent than surgeons, dentists, and nurses, more pampered than their predecessors,

6/ Dormer, "Plucking the Middle String," in *Our Domestic Landscape*, 15. See also in the same catalogue "New Jerusalem and the Domestic Landscape" for Dormer's polemical attack on British culture.

and worst of all, outside any "real" economy. Current craft, he bemoaned, was "seeking the apotheosis of uselessness – Art."[7] Dormer liked to quote the playwright Tom Stoppard: "Imagination without skill gives us modern art."[8]

7/ Peter Dormer, "The Appearance of Craft," *Craft History* 1 (1988): 80. This interesting journal, edited by the brilliant Justin Howes (1963–2005), lasted for just two issues.

8/ Quoted in Peter Dormer, "Beyond the Dovetail: Craft, Skill and Imagination," in *Beyond the Dovetail: Craft, Skill and Imagination*, ed. Christopher Frayling (London: Crafts Council, 1991), unpaginated.

For Dormer, design, craft, and morality were inextricably linked. His nine books (with two further books appearing posthumously), and his exhibition catalogues, talks, and articles, still read freshly, anticipating today's interest in a broader interpretation of craft, looking beyond studio craft and its various techniques and materials – ceramics or textiles, glass or metal or wood. Dormer would have sympathized with the expanded field presented in Richard Sennett's *The Craftsman* (2008) and the broad scope of the 2011 Crafts Council/V&A blockbuster exhibition "Power of Making," in which the studio crafts were overlooked in favor of 3D printers, customized prosthetic limbs, drystone walling, and hand-formed car panels. Reading Dormer today suggests that the strong identity of the 1980s and 1990s studio craft world, underwritten by the Crafts Council's exhibitions and publications, acted as both an inspiration – for Dormer admired the work of many individual makers – and an irritant. What is striking is the attention he gave to the studio crafts, in the form in-depth reviews of exhibitions and of fiercely argued attacks on individual makers.[9] His carefully articulated anger may seem unfamiliar today. We have, after all, witnessed a creeping abandonment of serious partisan criticism in specialized art, design, and craft publications and in the broadsheet newspapers. Current readers might mourn the current diminution of committed critical writing. But Dormer's attack on studio crafts' fine-art tendencies and his determination that the role of craft could only be a modest one now seem less relevant.

9/ See his brutal analysis of Ewen Henderson's fine 1995 exhibition "Pandora's Box": Peter Dormer, "Comment," *Crafts*, no. 138, January/February 1996, 48–49.

But it is still worth rereading Dormer, in part because the visual arts have developed in ways that he could not have predicted. Dormer would have been surprised at the explosion of popular interest in fine art and the fashionability of craft techniques and materials within that world, particularly in the context of ceramics. He would have been inspired by the development of pervasive computing and the ways in which 3D printing and cutting machines have integrated design and craft. He would have endorsed the renewed interest in vernacular craft in Britain, both rural and industrial.[10] He might, however, have been alarmed at the normalization of theory. Dormer believed that the pursuit of theory has desperately harmed art,[11] but I think he would have been interested by the emergence of theorized and highly creative craft scholarship that looks outside the studio crafts to embrace topics as various as crafts' role as a supplement to fine art, or the hidden story of craft within postwar Italian design, or the "differential" role of amateur craft, or the teaching of surgical techniques and the crafted nature of the Empire State Building.[12] From a sociopolitical perspective Dormer would have been horrified at the closure of so many material-based higher-education courses in the areas of ceramics, glass and metalwork, and jewelry, and amazed that such closures coincided with a government rhetoric endorsing practical skills and promising the expansion of craft-based apprenticeships, both cynically framed as panaceas for economic downturn and perceived social anomie.

The selection of Dormer's articles presented on the following pages belongs to a different world. At the time, the studio crafts had a much stronger presence and were seen by Dormer as a potential, if often unsatisfactory, antidote to the art world's abandonment of skill. And other kinds

10/ See Robin Wood, "Technology and Hand Skill in Craft and Industry," *Journal of Modern Craft* 4, no. 2 (July 2001).

11/ Peter Dormer, "Comment: The Appliance of Science," *Crafts*, no. 119, November/December 1992, 19.

12/ See Glenn Adamson, *Thinking through Craft* (Oxford: Berg, 2007), 9–14; Catharine Rossi, *Crafting Design in Italy: From Post-war to Postmodernism* (Manchester: Manchester University Press, 2015); Stephen Knott, *Amateur Craft: History and Theory* (London: Bloomsbury, 2015); Tim Dornan and Debra Nestel, "Talking, Touching and Cutting: The Craft of Medicine," *Journal of Modern Craft* 6, no. 1 (March 2013); and Ezra Shales, "Corporate Craft: Constructing the Empire State Building," *Journal of Modern Craft* 4, no. 2 (July 2011).

of craftedness found interesting by Dormer were overlooked and marginalized by commentators and institutions alike. He would have liked the fact that investigations of craft currently can encompass with ease two of his particular slightly tongue-in-cheek interests, flower arranging and dentistry.[13] Dormer would have celebrated the recognition by young design historians that craft culture is all-pervasive and deserving investigation wherever it can be identified.

13/ See Dormer, "Still Life with Flowers," *Crafts*, no. 110, May/June 1991, 46–47. The design world remains less imaginative: flower arranging was a central theme of the 2004 Design Museum exhibition "Constance Spry: A Millionaire for a Few Pence," causing the museum's chairman, James Dyson, to resign and ending with the departure of the director, Alice Rawsthorn. Since then the Design Museum, now in Kensington, has avoided any serious discussion of craft in any form.

Peter Dormer, "The Appliance of Science," *Crafts*, no. 119, November/December 1992, 18–19.

The Appliance of Science

Understanding how things work is one of life's pleasures. Critical writing and theory is one route to understanding, but we have probably come to overvalue theory. The prejudice in favour of theory is to be seen in science. For example, we have been sold the idea that in science, especially in modern physics, the idea comes first, then comes the device. That is arrogance says Joseph Schwartz, a physicist, in his book *The Creative Moment*. Schwartz gives many examples of successful practice preceding theory. The development of electric generators is one example: "There is nothing in the equations of electromagnetism that tells one how to make the things actually work."

This does not diminish the rôle of theory. On the contrary, reflecting theoretically on practical work can be immensely rewarding. Schwartz takes the steam engine as an illustration. In the eighteenth and nineteenth centuries, some very good engineers developed the steam engine into a sophisticated and accurate machine. However, the engineers, their clients and theoreticians began wondering if you could have such a thing as a one hundred per cent efficient steam engine. The answer is no, and it was discovered by Sadi Carnot, a French engineer, who worked out the answer by speculating in his head about an ideal steam engine. The ideal cannot, he concluded, be possible, and the encapsulation of his findings in the Second Law of Thermodynamics saved a lot of people a lot of fruitless work. It is also an example of a truth. No matter what your colour, gender, nationality or religious belief, the Second Law of Thermodynamics will hold, with or without your agreement.

Of course, not everything that is important to us can be generalisable into laws of nature. Critical writing in art and craft does not lead you to absolute generalisable principles, although it can achieve coherence and verification if what is said can be observed and agreed by other people.

Descriptive and critical writing, if not theory, has been quite important to the development and propaganda of the studio crafts. The writings of Ethel Mairet, Bernard Leach, Edward Johnston, Eric Gill and David Pye are examples of clear analyses based on observation and experience. Equally important have been the scholarly contributions of art historians, especially Michael Baxandall in *The Limewood Sculptors of Renaissance Germany* and, perhaps even more important, E H Gombrich in his *The Sense of Order*.

However, none of this very respectable thoughtful literature compared with the writing produced by art critics about art. The most notable difference between writing about contemporary art and writing about craft was that the former seldom, if ever, discussed techniques and methods of making or manufacture, whereas with craft the majority of writing – whether critical, scholarly, historical or journalistic – took technique and practice as a core element for review.

By the early eighties, a sense of urgency among some craft practitioners, teachers of craft history and others had grown, suggesting that not enough attention was being devoted to the "content" of the new craft. The argument that the crafts concentrated too much on technique and not enough upon ideas has been voiced in many places. In 1985 Audrey Walker, as Head of Goldsmiths' Textiles Department, wrote in this magazine that in textiles the primary importance was the idea and the intention: the discipline of making came second (*Crafts* No. 72).

Some years earlier, in 1982, a lecturer in the History of Textiles, Jacqueline Herald, wrote a long letter to the magazine (*Crafts* No. 55) criticising the lack of theory, and the absence of a critical vocabulary. She also questioned the sexist divisions that made what male artists did with textiles or paper "art," which if done by a woman was called "craft." She argued strongly in favour of women who were deliberately using the most decorative "techniques associated with women's domestic needlework in order to project a political and social statement." She ended her letter by saying: "At least my open-ended remarks may prompt some debate in the form of letters addressed to you. But should we be discussing such ideas in a magazine called *Crafts*?"

The apparent lack of critical interest in the crafts outside of the crafts world, and the apparent unwillingness of the general public to equate craft with ideas and mental – as opposed to manual intelligence – may have prompted some craft practitioners (Jacqueline Poncelet and Susanna Heron come immediately to mind) to decamp to the art world. Other craftspeople have since seen to it that catalogues accompanying their work contain intellectualising essays, setting the context of their work in the theories of art.

The revolt and complaint against craft, and against too much emphasis upon technique, has not always resulted in a demand for theory, but is sometimes couched in an appeal to the spiritual and the intangible. For example, the potter John Maltby wrote an essay called "The Leach Tradition" (*Crafts* No. 92). Maltby mounted a reinterpretation and an avant-garde rehabilitation of Bernard Leach by arguing that Leach had nothing to do with craft skill (a viewpoint which is a little at odds with Leach's *A Potter's Book* (Faber & Faber, 1940).

Here is an edited quotation from the article Maltby wrote for *Crafts* in 1988: "Leach was a bad craftsman when measured by any pre-industrial standard. His skills were inevitably underdeveloped and certainly inexact – yet he made, with Cardew, the finest and loveliest pots of this century. Pottery can be pursued at various levels, and technical expertise and dextrous skill are fascinating to watch and to acquire, but the life-force of a good pot lies outside such skill and knowledge. I do not suggest that such skills preclude creative vitality: rather they are an irrelevance."

To be frank, I think Maltby was writing nonsense, but at least Maltby has not excluded the object from discussion, and we can force him to begin to justify the argument empirically by comparing the pots of Cardew and Leach with other people's pots; also we can start a dialogue about what is meant by "life-force" by bringing the discussion back, again and again, to the pots in question.

The key writers of an earlier generation, being in the main practitioners, have retained the object, observation and empiricism at the forefront of their writing, and it would be immensely sad if critical writing and theories of craft and art began to dominate to the extent that objects produced are relegated to becoming cyphers for words. I sincerely believe this has happened in fine art. What has happened in art is the production of trivial objects whose main function is to act as theatre props for the essays that are written about them.

I believe in the primacy of practice: I do not think one should be ashamed of the word craft; I think that practical skill, and the practical intelligence involved in it, is fundamental to society and to the development of ideas. The pursuit of theory has desperately harmed art; other people are arguing that it has harmed other disciplines as well including, much to my surprise, physics.

Joseph Schwartz, whom I quoted earlier, has been dismayed at the division between experimenters (hands-on scientists) and theorists. He concludes: "Theorists today are so divorced from real experience of nature they have no unconsciously absorbed perceptual knowledge to draw upon. Everything they know has been learned from books. And the understandings based on this second-hand knowledge have inevitably been derivative and second-rate."

I think we must keep coming back to objects and the practitioners who make them, and test every word against them; we must also be willing – and able – to warn if we think things are going wrong. I certainly think there is a great deal that is right with the crafts, but I do worry about a slide into purposelessness as a number of craftsmen and craftswomen become what Schwartz calls "autistic" – cut off from having any real function or purpose.

For example, when I went to see the degree show at the Royal College of Art earlier this year, I was struck by the difference between industrial design and glass and ceramics. The industrial designers were looking outwards in terms of how other people would use their products. But, they were also looking outwards to how people would feel about their products, whether they would enjoy them. And, in thinking along these lines, the designers were also looking out towards the world of nature or of science and coming back with visual metaphors and similes and playful analogies. And, doing so in the light of knowing they were reaching out to other people. I did not notice evidence of this in much of the ceramics or the glass – the majority of which seemed inconsequential, cut off from any specific discourse or interaction with the rest of the world.

The general responsibility of a writer is to make things intelligible, and, for my own part, I am trying to map out (for myself as well as for any readers) what the current territory and content of applied art, studio craft and design amounts to. In a small, and I suspect largely unread, catalogue essay which was published earlier this year, I suggested the following as a sketch for a simple inventory of studio crafts today. Broadly speaking the studio crafts can be described as possessing four classes of object: functional; representational; naturalistic; and self-referential.

Functional craft: function provides a goal for the maker, a discipline for the work, and a conduit of understanding between the craftsman and the public. The craftsman or designer-maker is offering a useful object that has to be different in either design or aesthetic quality (or both) from that provided by industrial manufacture.

Representational craft: this is a craft which has function as a theme, but not as a primary aspect of its purpose. These objects are representative of function although they are next to useless. Large thrown jugs are an example; too big and too heavy for use, they use the theme of "jug" and of "domestic utensil" as their subject matter. The theme gives a discipline to the maker and an accessible content to the viewer/ purchaser. Ceramics especially abounds in such examples.

Figurative craft: this category includes ceramic animal and figure making, pictorial textiles and figurative wood carvings. The potential here is for naturalist interpretation or metaphorical allusion; the range can go from the decorative to the allegorical. Again, it is a category that is accessible to the public.

Self-referential craft: this is work in which function is neither present nor represented and it has no figurative or representational content. These works amount to examples of individual private languages.

The first three categories represent the sustainable core of studio craft, and a continuation of the development of practical intelligence; through which, and not in spite of which, ideas are developed and refined. Little that is intelligible can really be written about or discussed about the fourth category.

Peter Dormer, "The Future of the Craftsman, Part 1," *Art Monthly*, no. 71, November 1983, 36.

The Future of the Craftsman, Part 1

The concept of the "artist-craftsperson" is looking threadbare after just a decade. The artist-craftsperson is an unsatisfying and puzzling creature – born of a Civil Service neologist and a Conservative peer (Lord Eccles set up the Crafts Council in 1971) it now causes more embarrassment than celebration. During the 1980s the misfit will fade away but nonetheless, the underlying trend for the crafts is healthy provided it is resolutely allied with design and industry. The role and future of the designer-craftsman will be discussed next month.

The current voices for the fine art world – the newspaper critics and art journals – shun crafts. This attitude is understandable insofar as it is acceptable that such people and such journals stick to the easy option of judging crafts from the image presented by industry and its advertisers. For in this image the crafts are always presented as tending towards the picturesque and the reactionary. Indeed, the reactionary desire of wanting to exclude from one's personal life anything that might make it uneasy or unpalatable begets the desire for rosy, cosy picturesque-ness. Both qualities are the stock in trade of the mass manufacturers of "craft" objects (limited edition porcelain knick-knacks, for example) or mass produced "handcrafted" furniture (I see that Arthur Negus now fronts for a firm producing "traditional" fitted kitchens). This trade on "crafts" and "craftsmanship" is frequently a deceit with few of the objects being well made and most falling on the scale of mediocre to lousy. But trade in the picturesque is enormous and lucrative and especially popular with county and would-be county set people who live vicariously through porcelain hunting scenes and shammy brown Windsor furniture. There's nothing surprising in this embrace of the picturesque and the impetus towards cosiness is assisted through the fiction of replicas of the past. The quality of the wares is not so important and provided the consumer is told that this or that is *handmade* then imperfections (such as excess glue, daylight through the joints, ill-fitting lids etc., etc.,) are easily ignored – in any case, who challenges stage sets?

It is pertinent to note this comment from a Design Council report on the design of British consumer goods in which it discusses the relationship between designing large colour television sets and the British home market: "As 'pieces of furniture' the large colour sets are subject to the abiding characteristics of British home taste. Where people relax – usually the living room – warmth is paramount: cosiness and the elements of known comfort are solidly entrenched. The design of domestic furniture in the mass is a very, very slow transition back and forth between various interpretations of period: dark wood, patterned floral fabrics, traditional patterns or dull soft plain carpets ..."

Not surprising then that imaginative craftsmen and craftswomen sought a strategy which would distance them from the large reactionary rump of "crafts." The concept of the "artist-craftsman" which was really an oversight in the civil service draft papers submitted to Eccles when he was establishing the Crafts Council (or Crafts Advisory Committee as it began) was a Godsend – even though the evolution of this into "craftsperson" and "craftspeople" has turned it into a joke.

During the 1970s "artist-craftsman" became synonymous with the activity of making "one-off" functionless objects whose *raison d'être* was more often than not to question and then overturn every accepted norm of what a craft or craftsmanship might be understood to entail. In fact the "new wave" did not have a great deal to kick against that was worth the effort – they had the Bernard Leach tradition in pottery to rail against, they had the furniture of the Barnsleys and Gordon Russell to oppose but more than anything there was a need to put distance between themselves and the craft shoppe mentality. The art schools encouraged experimentation and innovation and with a few years, potters, weavers, and jewelers went rapidly through all the variations they could think of. In America ceramics went for a ride with such events as a performance recorded on video during which half-a-dozen idiots dunked their heads in slip (liquid clay) and then sat around waiting for it to dry.

But by no means all the innovations in ceramics or some of the other crafts can be so easily dismissed and indeed, whilst the decade of the "artist-craftsman-cum-craftsperson" has produced rubbish it has also produced some excellent decorative wares which are some way off their time for appreciation outside the craft/decorative art world. Nonetheless, the interpretation of the concept "artist-craftsman" that was given the most weight was the one which placed the emphasis upon the craftsperson as some kind of *contemporary* sculptor, painter or performance artist. The desire for art status was a part of the reason for this emphasis – the appelation "craft" was a handicap. Indeed a clear illustration of this is provided by the Sainsbury Centre's anxiety not to present its current exhibition of pots by Hans Coper as "craft" but as art, as sculpture. The assistant on the sales desk will tell you sniffily that the centre does not show "crafts." Coper's sculptural status is helped enormously by the fact that they are difficult to forge by prison craftspeople and that they each fetch several thousand pounds at auctions.

Until recently it was relatively easy for potters and weavers and others to act like "artists" in a trivial sense because all they needed to do was break craft conventions and keep ringing the changes. But all the time the worth of these innovations was judged in reference to crafts and not to work that was currently being pursued in sculpture. Thus whilst a textile "artist" might produce an "interesting" construction it was interesting more for the fact that a "weaver" had produced it and called it "weaving" than for anything else. (On the other hand it might also be said that people are more willing to point out the shallowness of craft objects than they are in fine art – more willing because they have fewer vested interests.)

A few men and women who began in the crafts have reached a stage where they and their work have left the crafts world altogether – which is to say they are prepared to have their work discussed in the same art historical contexts that contemporary sculpture or painting has to be discussed in. But for the rest it is likely that they will run out of innovations of the art-pastiche variety and will either recognize the legitimacy of re-working what they have learned into more mainstream functional or decorative ware or end up as full time teachers. Either way the day of the artist-craftsperson qua artist is nearly over because there was never enough substance in the concept to give it a permanent existence. This does not matter. Stronger trends are moving.

Peter Dormer, "Beyond the Dovetail: Craft, Skill and Imagination," in *Beyond the Dovetail: Craft, Skill and Imagination*, ed. Christopher Frayling (London: Crafts Council, 1991).

Beyond the Dovetail: Craft, Skill and Imagination

Towards the end of the exhibition "Beyond the Dovetail," I included a short section on non art crafts. Without wishing to descend into the sentimentalism of a Thought for Today homily I did want to put art and craft and the whole business of "self expression" into perspective. I therefore included reference to an AA Patrol, a juggler and a dentist as examples of different kinds of crafts in which imagination both aesthetic and moral was expressed through great skill. I could have chosen a hundred different trades and professions. And before plunging into the small pool of handicraft and studio craft I want to look briefly at one example of a non-artistic trade that nonetheless combines craft and imagination with aesthetic and moral values. I chose dentistry partly because it is underpinned by crafts such as ceramics and fine metal work.

David Harvie-Austin, a dental surgeon with a practice in Wimpole Street, London explains:

> A dentist must like working with his or her hands. Both gentleness and strength are required and one's actions must flow, one must be certain and one must be watchful – consider using a drill revving at a half million rotations a minute in the delicate wet smallness of the human mouth.
>
> Sometimes the dental surgeon is reconstructing a mouth and therefore concerned with function and appearance. Here the dentist is both structural engineer (literally) and designer. And one can understand that a dentist needs to have a logical mind and an imaginative one too (not all of us open our mouths to reveal a textbook problem). Patience, concentration and stamina are necessary.

One of the dentist's moral responsibilities involves alleviating pain but fulfilling this responsibility the dentist must, says David Harvie-Austin, "be both compassionate and dispassionate. You must sympathise with the patient's fear but not give way to it otherwise one's ability to operate is compromised."

One expects the crafts and imagination of a professional, such as a dentist, doctor, or surgeon as well as nurses and paramedics to be deep, complex and subtle because apart from mental pain nothing distorts a life more than physical pain. What shapes this work is the riskiness of it: the criteria for success and failure are observable, real, and not basically a matter of personal taste or opinion.

But the modern artist and craftsman can hide from risk in the thickets of opinion and taste. A lot of modern studio craft can only be judged on whether or not it takes your fancy and not on any hard factual criteria such as whether it is well made or whether it works well. "Well made" and "well functioning" are public, not private phrases. "Well made" entails an agreement among a number of people as to what bad making is. But in the case of many artefacts produced today, whether as craft or art, the communal vocabulary of good or bad makes no sense.

For example, in the exhibition there is a bowl by Ewen Henderson. Mr Henderson, a thoughtful man, has occupied for some years the no-man's land between craft and art. The vessel of his I have chosen is rough, volcanic and like a three dimensional lumpy water colour. I like it and I can imagine finding its aesthetic equivalent on a beach or in a scrapyard or in the base of an old tree.

However, it is less courageous an object than a box by David Pye or a jug by Mick Casson or a portrait terracotta by Neal French. These craftsmen are working with criteria that are publicly accountable – they are working with disciplines that have rules about good carving, good throwing and good making. These rules are not made up by the makers but are communal rules that exist, separate from each maker's whims and fancies.

Mr Henderson's work, like that of the other makers whose work I have displayed alongside his in the exhibition – Angus Suttie, Martin Smith, and others – can be discussed and it can be liked. But these vessels cannot be evaluated objectively by agreed criteria. Only these makers know whether they have failed or succeeded; whereas with French's portraits or Pye's boxes a lot of people can exclaim "Yes you have got it right here and here but you got it wrong there." It is the difference between "doing" religion and "doing" science: you can never get it "wrong" in religion, but you can get it wrong in science.

I think handicraft is important: it can be an expression of human care, thought, service and creativity but I believe it becomes all these grand things only through being channelled into specific goals which have criteria that can be assessed publicly. At a time when fine art appears to be inward looking and a matter of private concern to a relatively limited number of people it seems all the more important to raise the handicraft banner as an accessible, understandable and wholly honest public art or design form.

The very demonstration of craft skill is something that other people like to see, they can share in its triumph. The demonstration of skill, as much as imagination, is often evidence of the human mind at its best at work. The important characteristic of craft work is that craft (and the designs that bind it together) has communal roots. It is a perversity to make of craft a private language. Function, skill and tradition are not reactionary ingredients, they provide the bridges of comprehension between a maker and his or her public. Traditionally, craft, and its peer activity, design, have looked outwards, not in.

Yet what I here suggest as perversity has also been described as brave experimentation – turning craft on its head, doing away with skill and saying that since craft is not needed for its utility there is no need to use function as its guiding structure.

Some experimental work has introduced strong ideas, especially about design, into the applied arts – I think this is especially true of jewelry. But we can now see that over the years many of those feted for their bravery in experimenting have got stuck. They jettisoned skill and did not add to their knowledge, they have kept repeating variations on fairly shallow experiments and have limited themselves, not by lack of ability, but lack of knowledge.

They say: "Craft skill represses creativity." Yet the dullest work is unskilled.

They say: "Learning a craft is easy, it's thinking that's difficult." Yet in learning a complex craft it is the head that hurts, not the hands.

They say: "Art is about ideas, craft is dumb." Craft skill is a tool for exploring ideas or emotions in physical materials, without it "art" is dumb.

The main prejudice against craft skill is that it turns you into a technician or a mechanic and the prejudice against mechanics is that they are unimaginative. Is the practise of a craft skill – mechanical?

Is it true that what one wants is for skills to become embedded so that they are: on hand. If I have to go somewhere suddenly then I might take my car. I take my skill as a driver for granted, my skill is a tool, just as the car itself is a tool. Embedded knowledge becomes a part of one's identity. And as Edward Johnston, calligrapher and designer points out – to be good as a craftsman your ability in your craft must approach that of the mechanical. But there is a world of difference between approaching and being mechanical.

For those people who build or throw pots, model terracotta figures, paint portraits, play the violin or juggle balls in the air with grace there is likely to be a component of work, perhaps a large component, which approaches the mechanical.

In approaching the state of being mechanical one achieves knowledge over the tools, the materials and the subject matter such that one's ability to handle these elements becomes second nature but one does not subjugate one's imagination and mind to those skills.

For the good applied artist does not yield everything to the subconscious mind but remains consciously vigilant and ready to seize the opportunity of a chance occurrence and incorporate it into the design. Equally, of course, the thinking craftsman or woman will be on guard against errors; he or she will be ever watchful in order to protect the integrity of the design.

Craft skills are Janus faced. On the one hand, as more than one practitioner has observed:

"Skilled action implies control"
"Skill means: having a grip on the world"

On the other hand, having secured one kind of grip on the world, one holds on for dear life, too afraid to grasp the world in a different way. As a dull A level Art student I remember that, having found one way of drawing flowers, trees and other objects which involved a lot of careful cross-hatching, I kicked hard when another art teacher suggested drawing in paint on newsprint, rubbing charcoal and other rougher forms of drawing. And then I got a taste for the new possibilities they offered, became hooked and unwilling to try yet another but more analytical form of line drawing.

That is the danger of embedded skills: they become like much loved theologies. But this danger is not a reason for not acquiring skills.

Craft knowledge and imaginative thinking dissolve into one another like water into water to make for fluent, practical thinking. In the exhibition we have attempted to indicate something of this union by including a stage by stage break-down of the work by craftsmen and craftswomen such as David Drew, Mick Casson and Andrew and Joanna Young – we wish to reinforce the point that creativity flows through craft knowledge. Andrew Young made the telling point (telling because both he and Joanna are knowledgeable, skilled and imaginative in their designing) that "one never feels skilled enough to do what one is wanting to do."

David Drew designs and makes willow baskets; they are good examples of structural engineering (he understands engineering) and they derive their styling from the logic of function. Drew works by having a clear picture in his head of what he wants to achieve, he wants to make what he has imagined.

Apart from the soundness of structure he has as clear an objective in getting the shape, form and line of elements such as handle or rim right as has a letterer in achieving the right form for a letter in a particular alphabet. There are also functional criteria such as how easy and comfortable a basket is to hold and carry and whether it will distort with heavy loads.

Drew is not seeking "perfection" but that delicate balance between roughness and precision which is the magical middle ground of handcraft expressiveness. This balance is not achieved by accident.

The figurative craft of terracotta portrait sculpture as practiced by Professor Neal French raises criteria of a different sort. Neal French handbuilds his heads with coils of clay and then works on the features. There are three unforgiving sets of criteria: (i) Will the head stand up? It is a heavy vessel poised on a narrow neck and structurally it has problems. (ii) Is it a good likeness? There is no such thing as a good portrait head which does not look like the sitter – a head that does not look like its sitter is a failure. (iii) Does the head have something of the poise and presence of the sitter? (Waxworks often look like the people they represent but have nothing of their presence which is why they are lifeless.)

The potter Mick Casson is famous for saying that materials and processes are AS important as imagination (but not more). He makes, among other things, big, full-bellied salt-glazed jugs. His clays are carefully blended and the jugs are thrown in two stages. The belly and base are thrown first with 20 pounds of clay and at this stage there are choices such as where the centre of gravity is to be. If he chooses a high centre of gravity then the result is a high-waisted classical pot. When this stage is leather-hard then a hollow ring of wet clay is thrown to make the neck of the jug. Here choices include how wide the neck band should be and whether the jug is to become robust or refined. These are the sorts of choices that determine the pot's presence. Then the lip is pulled. After this the handle is added and again choices include how wide to make the handle and what the shape and depth of its section should be.

When the whole jug is leather-hard it is then decorated in coloured slips (liquid clay). Mick Casson usually dips his jugs. At this point he may decide to include a gestural decoration on the surface – maybe to give further surface articulation to the form by highlighting the neck or the sphere of the main body. The work is then given a biscuit firing and a glaze is added to the inside of the jug and then the second, most important firing begins. In this firing salt is thrown into the kiln and the sodium in the salt forms the distinctive speckled smooth glaze that gives an aquatint appearance to the pots. Even in loading the kiln there are choices to be made because where the jug is placed – including whether it is facing into or away from the fire (Casson uses wood-fired kilns with the flames licking and touching the pots) will affect the chemical transformation in the slip colours and a pot with the same slip may be fired a light blue or an almost inky black depending upon where it is situated in the kiln.

What links practitioners such as Casson, French and Drew is their implicit rejection of the doctrine of unrestricted individualism.

Unrestricted individualism is a blight in the arts and crafts because it puts up with accidental marks and forms or even arbitrary compositions. Moreover, there is little satisfaction for the craft or art buying public in being offered works that are at heart – compromised. They are compromised because the maker has no external goal to live up to or achieve – he or she can always, where the work is wholly individual, alter the composition or make do with a form rather than "get it right." There is no "getting it right" in work that does not relate to public values and a tradition.

The essence of talent – craft and imagination – is the ability to say, do, paint, pot, sculpt or weave that which you really intend. And there is another, important point to make here: the intentions themselves should have some value. The experimental studio crafts of the last twenty years are littered with "little" experiments, fleeting ideas that melt, meringue-like in the warmth of modest scepticism. To fulfill intentions you must have the craft with which to do so and you discover new intentions through the acquisition and continuous adding to your craft. The best craftspeople frequently feel they are not skilled enough – because their imagination is running before them and they are hunting the means to articulate it. That's the virtue of divine dissatisfaction over the meretricious.

Peter Dormer, "The Ideal Work of Vermeer's Little Lacemaker," *Crafts*, no. 93, July/August 1988. Excerpt from Dormer's essay in *Design after Modernism: Beyond the Object*, ed. John Thackaray (London: Thames & Hudson, 1988).

The Ideal World of Vermeer's Little Lacemaker

In this century the world's industrialised areas – in particular Scandinavia, Western Europe, Britain and North America – have sustained numbers of people who call themselves craftsmen and craftswomen. The persistence of the breed in the light of their marginal relationship to mainstream manufacturing is of interest. The irrelevance of craft work has caused it to mutate from being the livelihood of working-class artisans into an activity of self-expression for middle-class aesthetes or quasi-artists. …

The appeal of craft work

One of the most popular paintings in the Western world is *The Lacemaker* by Jan Vermeer, in the Musée du Louvre, Paris. This tiny painting (24cm × 21cm) of a young woman at work touches so many imaginations because it conveys that sense of perfect happiness which most people find when they too are, like the lacemaker, totally absorbed in an interesting activity.

The lacemaker is to be envied, and people argue that crafts workers are fortunate to have occupations in which they can "lose themselves." … To lose oneself in ordering and re-ordering one's work postpones the questioning of purpose and the setting of goals; and it is, after all, the setting of purpose and the striving for goals that makes men and women worldly.

In the past an approach to the local artisan for crockery or furniture or cloth entailed the same expectations of responsibility and service that we expect from a garage mechanic. … The notion of service in contemporary craft practice has become less clear-cut because the customer is no longer sure of his expectations and the maker has no very definite responsibilities … aesthetic value has replaced utility as the goal. What remains, however, is the question of whose taste becomes predominant – the "popular" taste of the consumer or the particular (and possibly recondite) taste of the individual maker.

In the 1950s and 1960s the crafts were supported by ordinary householders, not by museums. … The contemporary craftsperson was irrelevant as a producer of strictly functional wares, but became highly relevant when people wanted to add something to their homes that fed their eyes and their fingers. … This gave what the craftspeople were doing a genuine point. It was an act of service.

The post-war craftsperson was also peddling an ideology. … The ideal was to live from work that was one's own and done to the highest possible standard. It was a way of turning away from the structured routine of twentieth-century life.

The basis of the "alternative" wares economy is simple enough: the pots and other furnishings produced by a craftsman should look different from machine products. How they functioned, or even whether they functioned, was much less relevant. …

… in the early 1970s, especially in the United States and Britain … a new breed of craftsperson came into existence. This new craftsperson set up in opposition to his or her own craft. …

The economic structure for this quasi-art has been provided … by art school teaching, state museums purchasing for collections, the development of applied arts magazines, state grants and, especially in America, the existence of rich people willing to be persuaded by dedicated dealers and gallery owners that to buy the new craft was to buy the new art. …

[However, craftspeople's] attempts to make it as artists have been damned by the very materials they use. Media such as clay, glass and textiles are seen as archetypal craft media and people who work in them are automatically regarded as non-intellectual. In the contemporary fine art world any work which has a craft pedigree does not stand a chance of being accepted. Craft does not have intellectual connotations. True enough, the craftsperson has a position, but it is perceived as rural, reactionary, hidebound, skill-orientated and rooted in the ethics of toil and conservatism. This may be unfair, and it is certainly arbitrary. But what is and what is not "Art" is decided by the art world and so, without the acceptance of the art world, the concept of the artist-craftsperson will have no currency and has no currency beyond the pages of the crafts magazines.

Running to fat

The period of rule-breaking … in the crafts ended by the early 1980s. The contemporary craftsperson has attempted to find a niche half-way between handicraft and art. Some have been trying to re-establish the concept of the decorative or applied artist. Unfortunately, few of them willingly use the term "decorative" because they find it pejorative. They are surely wrong. It is surely an honourable title. …

The constraints and benefits of being a decorative artist are these: for the craftsperson it means that he or she is not expected to generate new insights into the world or to construct brilliant metaphors. Rather than lead the *avant garde* in art we expect craftspeople to use what art had discovered in order to embellish, for the pleasure of the rest of us, the home and civic and institutional buildings. It is a rôle which requires the craftsperson to use skill and be admired for it, but which also expects him or her to produce work that makes sense to the rest of us.

Unfortunately the rôle of craft as a decorative art has been corrupted by the rise of postmodernism. Whatever postmodernism is (or was?), it resists swift summary. … Suffice it to say that during the 1970s in the West there was a gradual loss of faith in several political ideologies (but especially Marxism). There was also a loss of faith in disciplines such as town planning and even economic planning. And there was greater caution about applying science to everyday life. …

Whenever there is doubt, uncertainty or fear people ring home to mother and in a sense that is what the architects and some designers have done: they have gone back to history and dug out things that have proved successful. Postmodernist art, architecture and design is not ashamed to use nostalgia as its dominant emotion. Almost all variations of classicism, Art Nouveau, Art Deco and a mish-mash of the Greek, the Egyptian and the oriental have been applied to the exteriors and interiors of buildings and influenced the design of the furnishings.

When the craftspeople, especially the Americans, saw what was happening they leapt to it. In glass, textiles and most recently and dramatically in furniture, they copied the postmodernist architects such as Michael Graves and Robert Venturi and attempted to outdo them. The craftspeople's reaction was, looking back, predictable, because craft, decorative art, having no intellectual impulse of its own, depends on other people for its energies and ideas. For example, for the first twenty years of the post-World War Two revival, the craftspeople of Europe and the USA were heavily dependent upon craft models provided by Japan and Korea. In America they also borrowed from abstract expressionism, then when Pop Art came along they seized on that, and when postmodernism came through there was no stopping them.

A combination of postmodernist excess and an ambition to be seen as an artist has tempted many a contemporary craftsperson into some highly skilled work of exaggerated design, size and complexity and hugely inflated prices. This phenomenon is most widespread in America, where there are more rich men and women prepared to buy the work for their new craft-art collections. The collections are frequently appalling and are, in essence, handicraft gone to fat.

In Europe, especially West Germany, Britain and France, there is … more of a nihilistic postmodernism styled up into a post-Holocaust chic of deliberately crude workmanship in foul materials. This work, too, is often both shallow and inflated. The work is supported, less by rich collectors, and more by contemporary museum curators.

Among those with a vested interest in craft there has been too much reluctance to admit that the world of craft is a world of modest ideas with a straightforward, commonplace vocabulary of familiar and functional forms which can be used purely decoratively. No pot or chair or table or glass vase can stand translation into a monument. The inherent modesty of craft is its strength. It is linked historically to the domestic environment. Perhaps the word "handicraft" should be resurrected. It is a word that serves to bring the craft ambition back to earth and allows us to affirm the link between craft and the home and not craft and the museum or the gallery. …

The function of craft in this stage of the twentieth century ought not to be the silly quasi-art funded by the ignorance of the *nouveaux riches* anxious to become collectors. It should instead be the art of familiar forms and understandable decoration for the ordinary home. Craft does not need to seek out a new decorative order: its main vocabulary – the variety of cosmetic artefacts, comprehensible to all – already exists. Craftspeople should concentrate on the fundamentals that are at the base of craft – service and truth to materials.

Handicraft and manufacturing industry

From time to time observers of the design and craft worlds are tempted (I am myself) to argue for a greater congruence between the craft aesthetic and the everyday one of mass-manufactured goods. We want to bring the craftsperson in from the outer margins of the opposition. In our more optimistic moments we new utopians see a marriage between crafts ideology, with its emphasis upon the expressive use of materials, and the manufacturing of everyday objects.

However, we seldom come clean as to what sort of objects we are talking about. There are, for example, a whole range of products, including electric kettles, irons, toasters, sandwich-makers, ovens, micro-wave ovens, dishwashers, washing machines, freezers, videos and television sets, where the craft aesthetic has no place. …

If not product design, then what about furniture and textiles? A combination of new technology and the craftsperson ought to make it possible for a rich variety of relatively reasonably priced furniture to be produced in small batches. However, to achieve this, the craftsperson would have to adjust his or her rôle and attitude, to spend creative effort in designing, not making. Secondly, he or she would need to abandon the workshop (except as a space for making prototypes) and do what the Italian furniture designers have done, which is to make use of a network of small but modern and well-equipped specialist businesses to make the various parts which are then assembled by someone else. The new craftsperson's rôle would be limited to overseeing the quality of the work. This approach is feasible but its disadvantages to craftspeople are that they lose the solace of a particular way of life in which pleasure is derived through the temporary loss of self in the all-engrossing act of making.

And so we always come back to the essential nature of handicraft activity: the pleasure of losing oneself in a practical activity offers a way of life which is different from that of the designer or designer-cum-overseer. The constituency of consumers necessary to support this way of life exists provided that the craftsperson does not default on the implicit contract of service that has evolved as craft has evolved in this century: the contract is to remain within the bounds of what is familiar and acceptable domestically. If these bounds are too restrictive, then the craftsperson can only seek fortune as a designer or as an artist – in worlds much tougher, more competitive and less tolerant of the gentle way of life depicted by Vermeer in his painting of the lacemaker.

THE REVENGE OF THE REVENGE OF THE PASTORAL REVENGE OF THE PASTORAL

GLENN ADAMSON

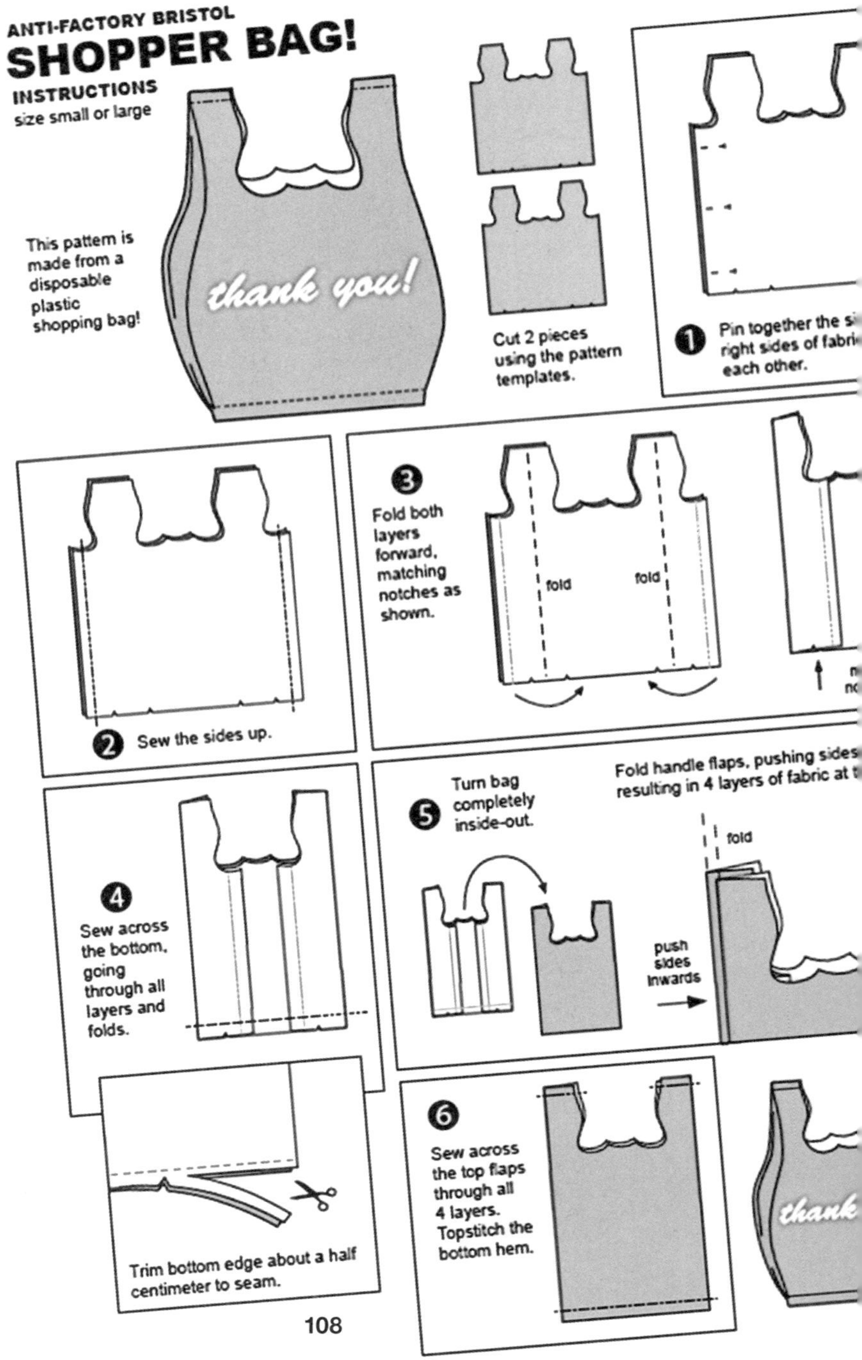
ANTI-FACTORY BRISTOL
SHOPPER BAG!
INSTRUCTIONS
size small or large
This pattern is made from a disposable plastic shopping bag!
thank you!
Cut 2 pieces using the pattern templates.
1 Pin together the si
right sides of fabri
each other.
2 Sew the sides up.
3 Fold both layers forward, matching notches as shown.
fold
fold
4 Sew across the bottom, going through all layers and folds.
Trim bottom edge about a half centimeter to seam.
5 Turn bag completely inside-out.
Fold handle flaps, pushing sides
resulting in 4 layers of fabric at t
fold
push sides inwards
6 Sew across the top flaps through all 4 layers. Topstitch the bottom hem.
thank

The Revenge of the Pastoral

Glenn Adamson

I got lucky with my first book, *Thinking through Craft* (2007). It found an interested audience, particularly within art schools, apparently striking a chord with makers who were tired of attempting to reframe craft as fine art and to elevate its status. This effort, though widely advanced, had proved mostly fruitless. I felt that craft's outsider status – which so many had considered a weakness – was actually a strength. Any attempt to elevate craft on terms that are premised on its exclusion was doomed to fail; but conversely, every instance in which craft was dominated, subsumed into a narrative of something "higher" than itself, was an opportunity for critique.

Looking back, I see *Thinking through Craft* as a young writer's book. It is somewhat disjointed, sometimes wandering away from its central theme. The five chapters attempt to accomplish very different things, and some of the arguments have been superseded. The last chapter on amateurism is thin stuff compared to Stephen Knott's full-length book on the subject,[1] and my tentative exploration of a feminist methodological base for craft studies, too, has been surpassed by the work of Julia Bryan-Wilson, Elissa Auther, and Jenni Sorkin.[2]

Some parts of the book seem to hold up pretty well though. One of these is the chapter on the pastoral, where I focused on craft's stereotypically marginal position with respect to dominant culture, its frequent association with rural or folk contexts. Even when found in an urban or industrial setting, craft is often small in scale, undercapitalized, and precarious. All of this makes it sound fragile, and one is forever hearing of craft's endangerment, with calls for artisanal trade to be rescued from the ravening jaws of modernity.

1/ Stephen Knott, *Amateur Craft: History and Theory* (London: Bloomsbury, 2015). I console myself with the thought that I at least advised Stephen when he was writing his doctoral thesis.

2/ Elissa Auther, *String, Felt, Thread: The Hierarchy of Art and Craft in American Art* (Minneapolis: University of Minnesota Press, 2010); and Jenni Sorkin, *Live Form: Women, Ceramics and Community* (Chicago: University of Chicago Press, 2016).

Stephanie Syjuco, *Anti-Factory*, 2014. Courtesy of Arnolfini/ Syjuco, Bristol.

There is, however, a counterintuitive sense in which modern craft's marginality is intrinsic to its power. Its position at the edge affords it an air of authenticity that the powerful lack by virtue of their political entanglements or overt intellectualism. Craft thus has a quality of honesty, enhanced by its association with tradition and the past, which can readily be equated to cultural depth. These attitudes lend craft an effectiveness that more centralized cultural practices miss.

The pastoral mode was already present in the ancient writings of Theocritus and Virgil, in which ideas were voiced by seemingly unsophisticated people, thereby giving them the ring of truth. The word pastoral derives from the Latin for shepherd (*pastor*), and many texts in the tradition feature characters literally tending their flocks while they engage in homespun philosophy. The modern craftsperson occupies an analogous position. By refusing the efficiency of industry and instead opting for a slower and more humane rhythm of labor, the pastoral maker not only lays claim to an independent system of values but reminds others what capitalism generally leaves behind.

This critical framework still seems useful today, but much has changed in the years since *Thinking through Craft* was published. Most importantly, the rhetorical use of the pastoral has shifted across the political spectrum from left to right. In the book, my key examples of the pastoral were rustic "dropouts" who detached themselves from the mainstream to assail its dehumanizing features. For these figures, craft served as a symbol of freedom and community.[3] The tide of the pastoral today, by contrast, is overwhelmingly conservative. It has found expression in nativist xenophobia – as in the propaganda leading to the 2016 Brexit vote – and has been central to other right-wing nationalist movements in Europe.

3/ See Elissa Auther and Adam Lerner, *West of Center: Art and the Counterculture Experiment in America, 1965–1977* (Minneapolis: University of Minnesota Press, 2011).

Pastoral rhetoric was also present in Donald Trump's efforts to present himself as an outsider speaking truth to power. When he surrounded himself with miners and hard-hat construction workers, presenting himself as their embattled spokesman, he was executing a familiar pastoral maneuver. This was obviously a con – as is now abundantly evident, Trump had absolutely no intention of helping anyone but himself – but the fact that the tactic worked so well, despite its flimsy armature, shows how readily the pastoral mode can be turned to reactionary ends.

These recent experiences are hardly unprecedented. Furniture designer and theorist David Pye once noted that fine workmanship has "doubtless been practiced effectively by people of the utmost depravity."[4] In keeping with this principle, the current generation of craft scholars has been more than willing to document the historical ties between craft and regressive politics. The association with nationalism, in particular, has been a major emphasis: fin de siècle "romantic" movements across Europe, the embrace of *mingei* (folk craft) ideology in imperial Japan, and the artisanal symbolism of the Italian fascists have all received extensive scholarly consideration.[5] Historians have examined positions that are difficult to locate on a conventional left-right axis, such as A. R. Orage's guild socialism.[6]

We can also see preliminary indications of the swing to populist pastoral in books like Matthew Crawford's *The Case for Working with Your Hands, or Why Office Work Is Bad for Us and Fixing Things Feel Good* (2009). The book reached a similarly wide audience as Richard Sennett's popular humanistic manifesto *The Craftsman*, published the previous year.[7] Neither was intended as a contribution to scholarly craft studies;

4/ David Pye, *The Nature and Art of Workmanship* (Cambridge: Cambridge University Press, 1968), 7.

5/ See Wendy Kaplan, ed., *The Arts and Crafts Movement in Europe and America: Design for the Modern World 1880–1920* (Los Angeles: LACMA, 2004); Kim Brandt, *Kingdom of Beauty: Mingei and the Politics of Folk Art in Imperial Japan* (Durham, NC: Duke University Press, 2007); and Yuko Kikuchi, *Japanese Modernisation and Mingei Theory: Cultural Nationalism and Oriental Orientalism* (London: Routledge, 2004).

6/ Adam Trexler, "Crafting a New Age: A. R. Orage and the Politics of Craft," *Journal of Modern Craft* 4, no. 2 (July 2011).

7/ Matthew Crawford, *The Case for Working with Your Hands, or Why Office Work Is Bad for Us and Fixing Things Feel Good* (New York: Viking, 2009); Richard Sennett, *The Craftsman* (New Haven, CT: Yale University Press, 2008).

Sennett's book is appealing for its sheer positivity regarding embodied skill, but it is vague in its grasp of artisanal processes. For the most part, he uses craft metaphorically, as a stand-in for care and social responsibility.

Crawford's book is more problematic by far. He is even more given to overgeneralization than Sennett, particularly in his condemnations of white-collar work. For instance, Crawford celebrates good honest motorcycle repair (his own adopted trade), but is casually dismissive of anything that smacks of hippiedom, referring to the hippie alter ego as "the wood whisperer with his hand planes, his curly maple, and his workshop on Walden Pond."[8] Crawford also presents a caricature of the heroic craftsman, implicitly male, who has no need to indulge in "chattering *interpretations* of himself to vindicate his worth."[9] His prescription for the twenty-first century – everyone should go get a goddamn real job and work with their hands – scarcely seems a practical proposal for prosperity in a rapidly digitizing, massively connected economy.

8/ Crawford, 85.

9/ Crawford, 15.

Crawford's book seemed cranky when it first appeared, but harmless enough. In retrospect, its enthusiastic reception was an ill omen. He bemoaned the corrosive effects of global post-industrialism and indulged in backward-looking fundamentalism and truculent anti-elitism. But who did Crawford imagine was designing, marketing, and distributing (or for that matter, buying) all those Harleys? Similarly, Trump had no interest in the practical impossibility and environmental undesirability of renewing the American coal industry. This narrowing of view, to take in only that which is picturesque and wish the rest away, is the very worst of the pastoral mindset.

All along, analysts have tried to offer correctives. "People think of coal mining as some 1890s, colorful, populous frontier activity," noted Mark Muro at the Brookings Institution in 2017, "but it's much better to think of it as a high-tech industry with far fewer miners and more engineers and coders."[10] One informative essay about Trump's widely publicized deal to save 1,100 jobs at the Indiana furnace manufacturer Carrier, seemingly an early win in his presidency, was succinctly subtitled, "Globalism Doesn't Give a Damn." The authors painstakingly detailed the cumulative effects of the rising tide of automation, the competition pressure of international labor markets, and manufacturers' dependence on the worldwide sourcing of materials and components.[11] The logic was irrefutable. Unfortunately, when it comes to not giving a damn, Trump and his followers were tough to beat.

In Britain, too, pro-craft statements in the pastoral mode emanated from the right side of the aisle; and here, too, there was an escalation from the merely unrealistic to the outright paranoid. In 2011, Chancellor George Osborne, perhaps envious of Germany's high-tech manufacturing base, closed his annual budget speech by calling for "a Britain carried aloft by the march of the makers."[12] In the years since, as British manufactures continued to decline, his call was picked up by other Tories, notably John Haynes, MP, who delivered a stem-winder of a speech at the Royal Society for the Encouragement of Arts, Manufactures and Commerce in 2015.[13] Hayes's presentation, a grab bag of contradictory propositions, echoed Osborne's embrace of skills as a means to economic uplift, and cited an unusual pantheon of aspirational figures – from William Morris (who would have despised Hayes's instrumentalism) to Winston Churchill (an "accomplished bricklayer").

10/ Mark Muro, senior fellow at the Brookings Institution's Metropolitan Policy Program, quoted in Hiroko Tabuchi, "Coal Mining Jobs Trump Would Bring Back No Longer Exist," *New York Times*, March 29, 2017, https://www.nytimes.com/2017/03/29/business/coal-jobs-trump-appalachia.html.

11/ Bryan Gruley and Rick Clough, "Remember When Trump Said He Saves 1,100 Jobs at a Carrier Plant? Well, Globalism Doesn't Give a Damn," *Bloomberg News*, March 29, 2017, https://www.bloomberg.com/news/features/2017-03-29/remember-when-trump-said-he-saved-1-100-jobs-at-a-carrier-plant.

12/ George Osborne, MP, budget statement, House of Commons, March 23, 2011. See also Larry Elliott, "March of the Makers Remains a Figment of Osborne's Imagination," *Guardian*, January 12, 2016, https://www.theguardian.com/business/2016/jan/12/march-of-the-makers-osbornes-economy-manufacturing-output.

13/ Andrew Walker, "UK Manufacturing: Whatever Happened to the 'March of the Makers'?," *BBC News*, January 26, 2016, https://www.bbc.com/news/business-35414075.

Hayes's stance was pure pastoral, decrying institutionalism and intellectualism in all its forms. "Too many things that are fundamentally practical have been given an academic veneer," he complained, as he cited bygone trades as the backbone of a healthy nation: "Within living memory, the butcher, the baker and the candlestick maker enjoyed significant social status, alongside the bank manager, the lawyer, and the schoolteacher. But these days, in most of Britain, the hard-won skill of individuals has been subsumed by brutal, impersonal ubiquity."[14] In Hayes's speech, the charmingly straightforward past damns the oh-so-complicated present. This would also, of course, be a critical maneuver in the successful Brexit Leave campaign – often tipping over into explicit xenophobia and racism.

14/ The Rt Hon John Hayes, CBE MP, "'The Craft So Long to Lerne': Skills and Their Place in Modern Britain," oral statement to Parliament, October 26, 2010, https://www.gov.uk/government/speeches/the-craft-so-long-to-lerne-skills-and-their-place-in-modern-britain.

This all adds up to a sizable blind spot in recent craft discourse. Ask most people in the field about craft and politics – whether makers, theorists, historians, or curators – and they are likely to think of examples like the pink pussy hats that stole the show at the Women's March in January 2017. "Craftivism" in all its guises has been a dominant topic in the field for years, invariably with a focus on symbolic practices grounded in leftist positions.[15] The phenomenon is certainly worthy of attention, but it should not mislead us into thinking that making things by hand is inherently progressive.

15/ See Faythe Levine and Cortney Heimerl, eds., *Handmade Nation: The Rise of DIY, Art, Craft, and Design* (Princeton, NJ: Princeton Architectural Press, 2008); and Maria Elena Buszek, ed., *Extra/Ordinary: Craft and Contemporary Art* (Durham, NC: Duke University Press, 2011).

In formulating a response, we first need to distinguish among "some versions of pastoral," to cite the title of literary critic William Empson's 1935 book. Empson distinguished between *simple* and *complex* variants within the pastoral mode. The former is reductive since it consists of little more than a presumption that tradition is good and change is bad. In simple pastoral, "the land"

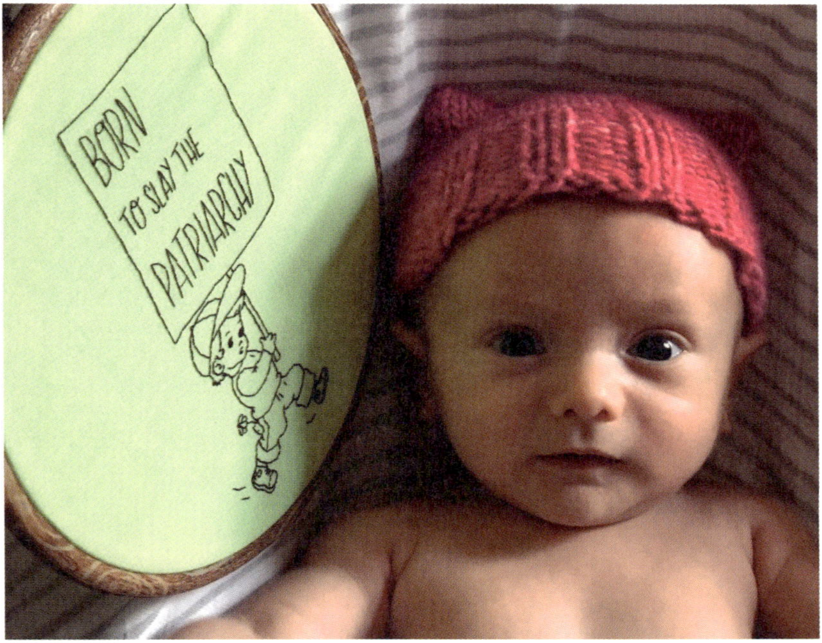

Women's March Pink Pussy Hat by Jayna Zweiman, and "Born to Slay the Patriarchy" embroidery by Shannon Downey, 2017.

is often figured as the wellspring – or, to cite the term favored by potter Bernard Leach, the "taproot" – of true authenticity. Within this type of construction, the past is simply a stick with which to beat the present.

Complex pastoral qualifies the same idea through attention to the basis of critique itself. Empson's model here was the Shakespearean fool who constantly makes allusions to his own status as a satirist. Complex pastoral speaks truth to power but recognizes its dependencies on power even as it does so (King Lear's fool, after all, is in the pay of the court). It is a way to articulate the gap between our search for authenticity and the contingent reality of any such claim. While anchored in the past, complex pastoral frames cultural memory as instructive rather than inhibiting.

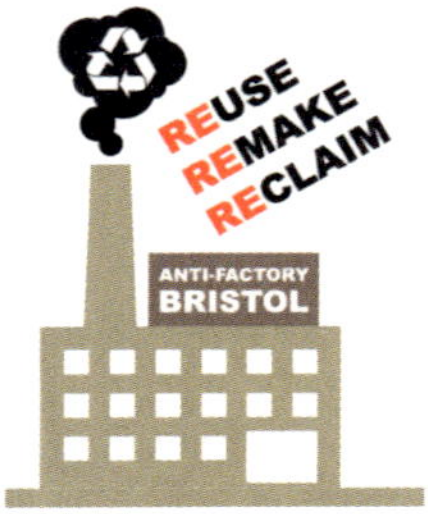

Stephanie Syjuco, *Anti-Factory*, 2014. Courtesy of Arnolfini/ Syjuco, Bristol.

Recent craft literature does offer models for self-awareness of this kind. Tanya Harrod's 2013 biography of the ceramicist Michael Cardew, *The Last Sane Man*, for example, portrays a man deeply at odds with the colonizing British administration of which he was a part; though a former apprentice of Leach, the two men neatly embody the dichotomy between complex and simple pastoral.[16] Contemporary artists such as Theaster Gates, Jeffrey Gibson, Allison Smith, and Stephanie Syjuco have established politically engaged practices in which making plays a complex pastoral role. The self-awareness they demonstrate is crucial, for the Left as much as the Right. When progressives employ simplistic rhetoric, they help to maintain a romanticism that can easily be turned in a reactionary direction. Treating long-established traditional practices as if they were of inherent value, regardless of their actual contemporary application, is all too compatible with right-wing nativism. Nor should we give in to the easy and reductive narratives of loss that are so endemic in craft discourse.

A related point concerns the figure of the industrial artisan, a tactical focus for the right wing, and one of the contemporary Left's most glaringly exposed flanks. This gap finds a parallel in craft historiography. As Edward S. Cooke Jr. has argued, the "long shadow" that William Morris casts over twentieth-century craft had many occluding effects; one of these was the near-total elimination of factory workers from consideration.[17] Morris's aesthetic proclivities meant that he did not recognize natural allies in the trade-union movement – the highly skilled so-called labor aristocracy, who may not have idealized the importance of joy in labor, but fought much more effectively for the rights of artisans than the reformers of the Arts and Crafts Movement ever did.[18]

16/ Tanya Harrod, *The Last Sane Man: Modern Pots, Colonialism and Counterculture* (New Haven, CT: Yale University Press, 2013).

17/ Edward S. Cooke Jr., "The Long Shadow of William Morris: Paradigmatic Problems of Twentieth-Century American Furniture," in *American Furniture 2003* (Milwaukee: Chipstone Foundation, 2003).

18/ Glenn Adamson, *Invention of Craft* (New York: Bloomsbury, 2013).

Recent scholarship has only just begun to redress this omission. Ceramics has offered one of the most appealing cases, with scholars such as Harrod and Ezra Shales and artists such as Neil Brownsword and Clare Twomey drawing long overdue attention to the high levels of skill and creativity present in industrial potteries.[19] In a deeply divided political climate, the question of who speaks for "blue-collar" people has become vital. The obvious answer, that they should speak for themselves, has generally not been embraced by politicians or scholars of any stripe. Material intelligence is deeply rooted among skilled industrial workers. Their perspectives should be right at the center of craft studies, not at the outskirts. The recognition of industrial skills can also help to redress the corrosive sense of disempowerment that nationalists and demagogues so effectively exploit.

19/ Tanya Harrod, "Studio Ceramics and the Factory: A Sketch," in *Things of Beauty Growing: British Studio Pottery*, ed. Glenn Adamson, Martina Droth, and Simon Olding (New Haven, CT: Yale University Press, 2017); Ezra Shales, *The Shape of Craft* (London: Reaktion, 2017); and Ethan Lasser, "Factory Craft: Art and Industry in Conversation," *Journal of Modern Craft* 6, no. 3 (November 2013).

This leads to the all-important question of strategy. Recent events inaugurated a dark time in cultural history, but one that now glimmers with the promise of widespread and effective political action, to a level not seen since the 1970s. Craft is a possible common ground because of its pervasive relevance to people in many walks of life. Protest is great, but it is not enough; as I argued in my recent book *Craft: An American History* (2021), making is a means to bind together our fractured societies.[20] If the pastoral mode is to be effectively used, its comfortable clichés must be avoided. The assumption that craft's natural place is within safe confines, or at the margins, needs to be abandoned. The skilled maker does not need to be a silent helper in the wings, or a proud figure within an isolated tradition. Skill is a form of power, with all the responsibilities that power entails.

20/ Glenn Adamson, *Craft: An American History* (New York: Bloomsbury, 2021).

In addition to makers themselves, others involved in craft discourse must also stress those aspects of making that connect people and cultures, rather than those that smack of retreat. Craft should never have been put in the dimly lit recesses of culture in the first place, and there is no reason to reproduce that error now. We will have to abandon the presumption that artisanal skill is inherently oppositional, a holdout against an imagined, unitary, impersonal "mainstream" culture. This has been a long-standing, cherished, and powerful dream. But now, it's time to wake up.

Theaster Gates, *Afro-Ikebana*, 2019. Cast bronze, clay, tatami mats. Photo by Theo Christelis, White Cube.

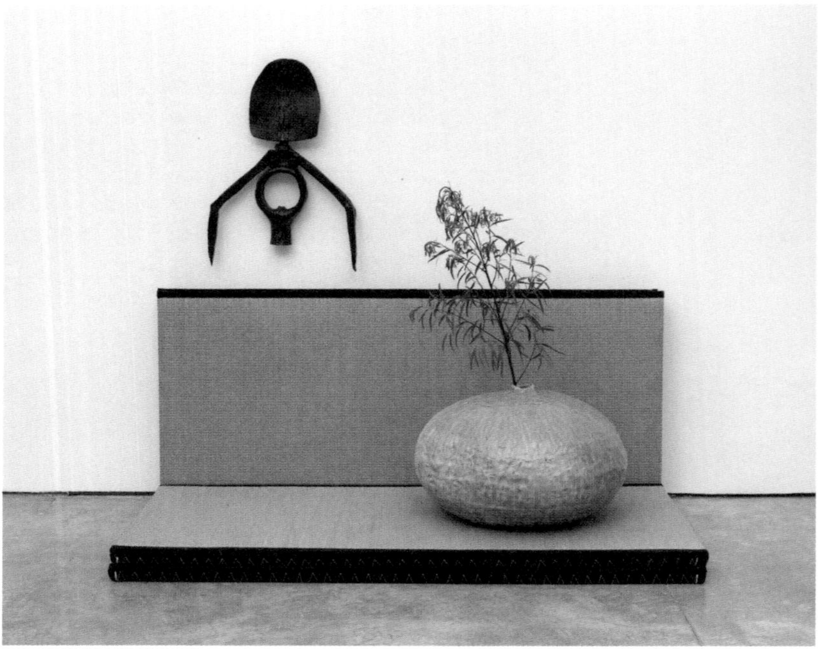

AFTER THE CRISIS OF VALUE: SOME FURTHER REFLECTIONS ON SKILL AND DE–SKILLING

JOHN ROBERTS

John Roberts

A version of this essay was presented at the Städelschule, Staatliche Hochschule für Bildende Künste, Frankfurt am Main, January 18, 2017.

In Homer's *Iliad* we encounter perhaps one of the greatest manifestations of preindustrial craft and artisanal skill: the manufacture of Achilles's new shield and armor by Hephaistos, which was needed to defeat the Trojans after Achilles agreed to return to the fighting during the Trojan war. Visited by Achilles's mother, Thetis, the wife of Peleus – a mortal not a God – the banished and lame god Hephaistos (condemned to a nether life of labor in his foundry) is asked to create a magnificent shield and set of armor surpassing all others. Thetis says, "I have come to beg at your knees, hoping that you will give my doomed son a shield, a fine pair of greaves with ankle pieces, and a corselet."[1] She does not have to beg, however, because she is much loved and admired by Hephaistos, after taking him in as a young disabled boy and bringing him up. Hephaistos is pleased to be able to at last repay what he calls "the debt of life," and to make a set of armor, "such that all the many men who see it will marvel at the sight."[2] And so he sets to work immediately while Thetis is there, getting all twenty of his bellows to blow at the same time. He then throws bronze, fire, tin, gold, and silver on the fire, before gripping a mighty set of tongs in one hand and a hammer in the other:

1/ Homer, *Iliad*, trans. Martin Hammond (London: Penguin, 1987), 306.

2/ Homer, 306.

> First he began to make a huge and massive shield, decorating it all over. He put a triple rim round its edge, bright and gleaming, and hung a silver baldric [belt or shoulder sash] from it. The body of the shield was made of five layers: and on its face he elaborated many designs in the cunning of his craft.
>
> On it he made the earth, and sky, and sea, the weariless sun and the moon waxing full, and all the constellations that crown the heavens, Pleiades and Hyades, the mighty Orion and the Bear, which men also call by the name of Wain:

she wheels round in the same place and watches
for Orion, and is the only not to bathe in the Ocean.

And so on it he made two fine cities of mortal men.
In one there were marriages and feasting, and
they were escorting the brides from their houses
through the streets under the light of burning
torches, and the wedding-song rose loud.[3]

3/ Homer, 307.

And on and on this tour de force of depiction and mimesis on the shield goes. In the first city, two men are quarrelling over blood money for a man who has been killed, with people shouting their support for each man; above the crowd, elders are seated in judgment on the fate of the two men; and two talents of gold lay on the floor, waiting to be claimed by the successful petitioner. In the other city, two encamped armies stand outside the city, the defenders, women, children, and old men on the walls, the young men are setting out to meet the armies, clashing on the banks of the river with bronze-tipped spears. This is set on a field, with teams of plowmen pressing onto the headland and back, on land where reapers are at work; three sheaf-binders are ready to receive the cut corn from boys behind them, looked on by the king holding his scepter, with his heralds nearby preparing a feast. Next to this scene is a vineyard, with grapes made of gold, the poles supporting the vines made of silver, and a fence made of tin, populated by girls and young men carrying the crop in woven baskets and a boy playing a lyre with revelers behind him. Alongside this scene are cows, four herdsmen, and nine running dogs, and in front of the cattle there are two lions that have killed a bull and are gulping its black blood, all accompanied by white sheep in a beautiful valley. Next to this scene there is a dancing floor on which young men and women are dancing, watched by a large crowd. Finally, running around the rim of the shield, is the mighty Ocean River.

The sheer luxuriant skill and inventiveness demonstrated, which is contained within the relatively small space of a shield, is clearly, for Homer, a gift from the gods. As Achilles says on receiving the shield from his mother, along with a corselet "brighter than the light of a burning fire" and a "beautiful finely-worked" heavy helmet with an added golden crest on top that "no mortal man could have made."[4] Yet if the shield is the work of the gods, nevertheless, it is not an act of supernatural legerdemain or magic. Homer clearly shows Hephaistos in the act of making the shield, of utilizing his skill and strength in the foundry to produce something that takes on the character of ordinary human creativity and endeavor. The *Iliad* was written during the Iron Age, a time when the status of the metalworker was extraordinarily high. The smith was celebrated for producing things of great beauty and strength from mere inert, undistinguished matter, and, of course, for making the everyday tools and symbols of a martial culture and a permanent war economy. In this light, the ancient smith in myths and stories in this period, from Tibet to Ireland, is seen as the great nurturer of things and people, particularly of the hero of the story. In *The War That Killed Achilles* (2010), Caroline Alexander says that it is the smith – the forger of things and lives – "who makes safe [the] young hero, fostering him and serving as his guardian."[5] Hephaistos is the great protector of lives.

4/ Homer, 310–11.

5/ Caroline Alexander, *The War That Killed Achilles: The True Story of Homer's Iliad and the Trojan War* (London: Penguin Books, 2010), 15.

The notion of craft skill and artisanal prowess nurturing the community, the polity, is of course central to the nineteenth-century capitalist valorization of the premodern craftsman, even if the focus is less on blacksmith and martial crafts than the work of the church artisan – the carver of stone – and the woodworker. Looking back to the achievements of the medieval guilds, John Ruskin, Karl Marx, and William Morris all saw the would-be integral skills of the medieval craftsman as a defense against the alienation of workers' skills under capitalism's transformation of labor into labor power. But this is precisely a defense, and in Homer's vision the artisan was a productive forger of lives. Craft skill for Ruskin, Morris, and Marx, under the increasing pressure of the division of labor, was a way of protecting the individual worker from this state of alienation, as much as serving the community. As Marx said famously in *The German Ideology* (1845–47): "Medieval craftsman [...] had an interest in their special work and in proficiency in it, which was capable of rising to a limited artistic sense. For this very reason, however, every medieval craftsman was completely absorbed in his work, to which he had a complacent servile relationship, and in which he was involved to a far greater extent than the modern worker, whose work is a matter of indifference to him."[6]

6/ Karl Marx and Friedrich Engels, *The German Ideology*, in *Marx and Engels: Collected Works*, vol. 5 (London: Lawrence & Wishart, 1976), 66.

This, then, is the condition of the laborer under the modern division of labor and the accumulation of capital: without recourse to the protection of some kind of integrated craft skill, the worker is invariably exposed to a process of labor that diminishes or erodes his or her self-esteem and, therefore, his or her subjectivity. In other words, craft skill in these terms – protected inside guilds or unions – secures the individuation of the worker, namely the interrelationships between hand, intellect, self-development, and social identity. This was a powerful vision, certainly up until the 1960s. But, of course, the protection of craft skill does not challenge the servile relationship between the laborer and the master – there is no protection against masters – or ameliorate the conditions of those laborers engaged in repetitive, backbreaking, manual labor. Craft skill is, rather, the privileged apex of the productive process, and directly vulnerable to the development of manufacture in the cities of the nineteenth century. It is the skills of these workers that will either be abstracted into the workings of machines or assimilated into the abstractions of large-scale production processes.

Under the continuous refinement of the division of labor in the second half of the twentieth century, the dissolution of "complex labor" into "simple labor" (de-skilling), effects a radical separation between the fast-changing and residual skills of the worker (the machine operator and facilitator, the factory hand, the overseer) and the notion of labor as a source of craft individuation. There is, therefore, little sense that craft skills – even defended from within the space of the unions – have the capacity to protect the worker from this process of abstraction. Skills are eroded, destroyed, re-functioned, and simplified, abstracted into machines (robots) in a continuous process of de-skilling rather than in a process of de-skilling and re-skilling. Harry Braverman argued in *Labor and Monopoly Capital* (1974) that this process is inexorable for workers.[7] New skills across industries may indeed be created, just as new industries come into being (the building and maintenance of robots today, for example) and older industries pass out of existence, but across the working class as a whole, these new skills are largely residual, or even not skills at all, instead being mere forms of facility. What new skills are created as a result of technological and technical innovation are those taken up by technicians and executives, who as a result have a greater knowledge of the productive process overall than the old collective worker. This is why the vast majority of jobs created today for workers are invariably low-skilled or "no-skilled." Marx saw the beginnings of this process already in the 1860s in his reflection on the increased inputs of science into the production process in

7/ Harry Braverman, *Labor and Monopoly Capital: The Degradation of Work in the Twentieth Century* (1974; repr, New York: Monthly Review Press, 1998).

8/ Karl Marx, *Grundrisse*, trans. Martin Nicolaus (Harmondsworth: Penguin, 1970).

the chapter "The Fragment on Machines" from *Grundrisse*.[8] Although in *The German Ideology* Marx praised the work of the medieval craftsman as a source of craft integrity, he knew that the alienation of labor under the relentless violence of the division of labor, and the growth in the organic composition of capital, would not be solved or healed by a defense of the craft integrity of labor. This did not mean, for him, that a defense of what remains of craft skills was obsolete, but rather that the celebration of craft skills, as in the romantic anti-capitalism of Ruskin and Morris (and even Hans-Georg Gadamer and Martin Heidegger after the Second World War) was not the key to the de-alienation of workers and human emancipation. For Marx, the struggle of the worker for autonomy was a struggle over time: the dominance of free labor over necessary labor; the securing of labor free from the linearity and time-as-measure of the value form; and, therefore, the freeing of labor from labor power.

This shift from the question of skill and de-skilling within the cyclical framework of boom-and-bust to questions more precisely of time and value within the growing crisis of labor defines our present period. This is why the "end of work" has become crucial to recent radical political theory – from André Gorz to *Endnotes*, Nick Srnicek, and Alex Williams – because the exponential rise of de-skilling, the robotic displacement of living labor, and consequently the detachment of unemployment and underemployment from so-called business cycles have made the question of free labor a political and emancipatory priority.

Lack of available jobs is always good for capital, because it keeps down wages and disciplines labor, but now global structural unemployment and underemployment threatens the stability of the system as a whole. And no more so than in relation to the uncontrollable character of the growth of the reserve army of labor itself – or the rise in surplus populations – with the incorporation of working populations in Africa and Southeast Asia into the global workforce. This massively increases the available pool of labor in a labor market where there are too few jobs. In turn, the jobs that are conceivably available to such workers are themselves disappearing under the onslaught of robotics. It is predicted that something between 47 to 80 percent of current jobs will be automatized in the next twenty years, and these jobs are not simply in the low-skilled service and manual sectors, they stretch into the administrative domains of law, medicine, engineering, and insurance (a Japanese insurance company, for instance, has recently replaced its staff who determine payouts to policyholders with AI machines). Two forces, then, are meeting in this current period: the secular tendency for capitalism to produce surplus populations that cannot be absorbed by the labor market, and capitalism's immanent tendency to destroy living labor in pursuit of profits and cost effectivity. The result is that an increasing number of workers are superfluous to the needs of capital. In the advanced economies, this has forced many workers into improvised and impoverished self-employment, or into hour-by-hour punitive zero contracts living off poverty wages; in the so-called industrializing economies, this is reflected in the increased participation of workers in the growth of noncapitalist subsistence economies.

The crisis of waged labor, then, is not the epiphenomenal effect of cyclical underemployment, it is rather the structural consequence of capital accumulation, and accordingly, not just identifiable with the rationalizations of neoliberalism. On the contrary, since the 1970s neoliberalism has been the bitter crisis management of this intractable reality and the fiction of full employment. In the long term, growth will continue to slow down and stagnate, non-job recoveries will continue to be implemented as a placebo effect, and job precarity and short-term contracts will increase – all in a context where "work" for the majority is no longer seen as a source of pride or emotional investment. Of course, workers' dissociation from their identity as workers does not begin with neoliberal precarity. The crisis of the self-identity of the worker as a worker is increasingly visible in the 1940s and 1950s, and alienation is indivisible from waged labor from the very start of the factory system. Yet, with this conjunction of forces in the current period, social atomization, precarity, stagnating wages, and increased surveillance at work has profoundly changed the relationship between waged labor and workers' self-identity. Workers' alienation is no longer mediated by collective use values that workers have a modicum of control over in the factory and identify with as a set of "common goods" outside its gates. As *Endnotes* asserts, increasingly "workers [can] no longer see themselves as building the world in the name of modernity or a better, more rational world. On the contrary, that world [appears] already built, and [is] entirely out of their hands."[9] But we should not confuse this knowledge simply with a rise in cynicism or pessimism. The crisis of work in the wake of the global contraction of waged labor has passed beyond that. Rather this awareness reflects the real conditions under which workers labor, and the value of labor itself represents the actual internalization of the self-undermining tendency of the capitalist mode of production. Even in jobs that are reasonably well remunerated or have a high social status, there is a feeling of how pointless and self-serving the work at hand is, when relentless drives for efficiency and cost saving prevent the job from being done

9/ "A History of Separation," *Endnotes*, no. 4 (October 2015): 146.

properly or at all. As Peter Fleming puts it, "The prototypical neoliberal manager requires social goods to attack – something to bite – even if this results in major organizational dysfunction."[10] That is, the conflict between exchange value and use value appears to be inhibiting the reproduction of labor power itself. In a world of unattainable targets and efficiency, there is a growing surplus regulation of the working day that compensates for this crisis of targets and efficiency. To quote *Endnotes* again: "Social life continues to be founded on the exchange of labours; yet with the extension of the fixed capital base, labour is no longer key to production. Direct human labour plays an increasing subsidiary role in production."[11]

10/ Peter Fleming, *The Mythology of Work: How Capitalism Persists Despite Itself* (London: Pluto Books, 2015), 97.

11/ "A History of Separation," 184.

The continuing crisis of work over the last thirty years, therefore, has huge implications for thinking through the content of labor faced with the crisis of labor power. In a world in which the de-skilling of work is now accompanied by tireless surveillance and targets and the collective worker as a living source of opposition has collapsed, the idea of reskilling as a way out of this impasse of capitalism's immanent destruction of living labor is a fantasy. The dialectic between skill, de-skilling, and reskilling has broken down; the cost of the development and refinement of knowledge in production is now the implementation of restrictive skills over extensive skills. For example, the introduction of driverless cars, vans, and trucks over the next twenty to thirty years will remove the driving skills of millions from production and everyday life. Many may welcome this, given that this change could – as is claimed – reduce car accidents exponentially. But again, it disconnects the laboring (and nonlaboring) body from the development of learned skill and practice, as if all collective skills were an affront to the greater demands of consumption and machine efficiency.

In the light of the above, then, it is no surprise that to offset this, management ideology seeks to import some notion of creativity from art into the workplace and work relations. In a world of relentless de-skilling – of the transformation of skills into routine facility – the idea that you and your coworkers might be involved in an autonomous free exchange of ideas is obviously deeply appealing. From Luc Boltanski and Ève Chiapello to Maurizio Lazzarato and Antonio Negri, much has been written on this soft-management model as the integrated obverse of the punitive neoliberal regime of targets and efficiency.[12] There is not the space here to discuss this in detail; suffice it to say that what is important about this shift is how the critique of instrumental labor – a critique obviously so central to modernism and the modern movement and twentieth-century Marxism and critical theory – has entered the domain of productive labor itself. Of course, it has merely entered it and not transformed it in the way the Soviet Constructivists hoped. Yet it reveals what the crisis of work imagines for itself in the period of capitalist non-reproduction: a phantasm of frictionless free creativity built on an image of art as a realm of self-transformation. This creativity is, however, as instrumental as the one that it seeks to replace: it abjures critical thinking whenever creativity-as-critical-thinking actually works to shift practice in a radically democratic and postcapitalist direction. As William Davies has argued recently: "One way of interpreting the apparent senseless violence of punitive neoliberalism is as a strategy for the circumvention of crisis and, at the same time, an avoidance of critique. In place of critical forms of knowledge, which necessarily represent the deficiencies

12/ For a discussion of this issue, see John Roberts, "Labor, Emancipation and the Critique of Craft-Skill," *Journal of Modern Craft* 5, no. 2 (July 2012): 137–48.

of the present, forms of empty affirmation are offered, to be repeated ritualistically. These lack any epistemological or semiotic aspiration to represent reality, but are instead ways of reinforcing it."[13]

13/ William Davies, "The New Neoliberalism," *New Left Review*, no. 101 (September/ October 2016): 132.

Creativity in the workplace, then, has become a populist managerial mantra for the avoidance of critique at the workplace and elsewhere, a way of generating a consensual image of worker participation and free exchange. Even if most workers know the limits of such creativity, the notion of the workplace – particularly the new creative-industries workplace – continues to have a certain allure in the new digital economy, especially for artists who ironically see an opportunity to find a working space – and wage – outside the often wretched conditions of practice. Indeed, this is one of the strange ideological anomalies of the current crisis of work. The willingness on the part of a growing sector of artists to either collaborate with the new cultural industries as part of a team or as an individual consultant, or align their artistic identity altogether with the instrumental objectives of a commercial enterprise as an employee, is cause for concern. Of course, there are good reasons why this is happening, beyond the expediency of paid employment or even opportunism.

Contemporary artists are no different from productive and nonproductive laborers in being subject to a process of de-skilling as a consequence of changes in the relations of production. But if art has lost some of its artisanal, productive allure over the last fifty years as a consequence of this, this does mean that artists are objectively excluded from artistic production on the basis of these changes. De-skilling is never absolute, because, as free labor, it is detached from the discipline of labor power: artists do not make their work under the constraints of the value form and necessary labor time and, consequently, a given template. They are not under threat of going out of business because they don't meet the average costs of labor inputs per unit; artistic labor, then, is not governed by the average time taken by all artists to produce a given commodity. Artists can take years to make one piece of work, and will not be punished by the market for the sale of artistic commodities for doing so. "You've taken too long, so we'll find someone else!" Yet if artistic free labor is not subject to the value form, it is subject to the generalization of social technique across industrial and nonindustrial production. Given the implementation of the computer as a universal tool across all sectors of production, the skills, techniques, and resources that artists use today are very similar to the skills, techniques, and resources that workers in the cultural industries, service industries, and administrative sectors use. This means there is a general convergence of technique across the artistic and nonartistic sectors; artists, cultural-industry workers, and administrators image and text search, file share, edit, montage. For a number of theorists – including Antonio Negri, Paolo Virno, and Maurizio Lazzarato – this is a positive development, in a way echoing the communization of technique debates in the early years of the Soviet avant-garde. And many artists have followed them in this assessment, seeking to hire out their "conceptual" and digital skills to companies as the basis for establishing a new relationship between art and business. This naturally has some appeal to the artist, who believes their commitment to art beyond the gallery might find a new home in the would-be "social agendas" of corporations or start-ups. However, the immediate consequences of this move are self-evident: there is no room for artistic free labor in the enterprise (as the Productivists found in the factories they entered in the early 1920s, even though they were run by "red" managers). All use values in the end are subject to the competitive demands of the enterprise, and therefore are invariably captured by the instrumental ends of the value form, even when labor inputs are not measured strictly hour by hour in the workplace itself. The assumption that the convergence of technique across the art/nonart divide under the expansion of general social technique is unambiguously positive is therefore a myth. Indeed, if the artist is to retain their critical or autonomous relationship to technique they must resist the subsumption of their labor under abstract labor, because abstract labor is qualitatively different from artistic labor – in terms of means and ends – and therefore antithetical to anything resembling creativity as critique. Even if neoliberalism would assume otherwise, technique is not another name for social adaptation. On the contrary, it is also defined by interdisciplinarity and noncompliance.

This is where Homer and Hephaistos come back into view. Not because Hephaistos's dexterity and abundant skills offer a comfortable image of creativity in times of cultural ruin and crisis. There is no going beyond general social technique and a return to the artisanal; there are no longer images of godlike creativity available to the artist this side of bathos, hysteria, and laughter, that is. In a sense this is all obvious: Hephaistos is not a figure for our times; someone who, armed with tongs and a hammer, can drive away the violence of abstract labor. Nevertheless, the excess of his creativity should give us pause for thought in light of the subsumption of artistic labor under abstract labor. What is striking about Homer's presentation of Hephaistos's superhuman creativity – if we read it with a degree of philosophical thoughtfulness – is that the shield becomes a kind of compressed Gesamtkunstwerk. This does not mean the shield is some ancient version of "art in the expanded field" or some premodern Wagnerian spectacle, neither is it a metaphor for the hive mind in network jargon or creativity as an open river, but rather it is something close to *Bildung*: the enactment of a critical community in which the free exchange of the labors of the many are represented by an infinite overlapping of ideas in a confined "conceptual space." And this, essentially, is the epistemological horizon of the artist today, confronted by the capture of their skills by abstract labor, or its crass opposite: the fleeing of the artist back into the artisanal and the anti-theoretical miniaturism of art-as-craft. To sustain their autonomy – that is, to sustain the interdisciplinarity of technique – the artist must, in a sense, subject themselves to the decentered critical labors of a living and open research community. A research community, therefore, that defines its relationship to knowledge as external to what the artist might contribute to the knowledge industries; a research community of multiple projects that defy the market rationalization of "outputs" and "impact." For it is the artist's submission to the demands of infinite ideation as a condition of the free exchange of art's labors that will determine what skills are worthy of the name of art.

POST-STUDIO CERAMICS CERAMICS CERAMICS CERAMICS CERAMICS CERAMICS CERAMICS CERAMICS

CLARE TWOMEY

Clare Twomey

Questions of object, people, skill, and purpose inform my thinking, together contributing to the development of "Factory: The Seen and the Unseen" at Tate Modern in 2017. For one week, the Tate Exchange was transformed into a working factory, where everyday objects were made from clay to explore ideas around the concept of production. The project consisted of a thirty-meter production line, forty factory staff, eight tons of clay, a wall of drying racks, and over two thousand fired-clay objects occupying the entire fifth floor.

The purpose of the work was to explore an idea of the factory that refers to shared labor, where the production line is composed of many parts and processes, and through shared goals a product is completed. The factory, which was built for Tate Exchange, was not a real factory or a real place of work, but rather a place of simulation intended to draw us into a conversation about how we connect to our everyday ideas of labor, value, and exchange. The factory drew the viewer into the rhythm of the tasks of labor, the enchantments of handling materials, the languages of labor and skills and craft in repetition, and the development of knowledge.

The following week, the redundant factory was instigated. The workers were gone but their voices remained through a series of recordings made during production. The machines, the materials, the benches became small monuments. The space was filled with the evidence of the human, but the wholeness of the factory was fractured. A new space came into being where the human was craved. The factory became a proposition of both loss and potential. The tasks of labor were to listen, reflect, and observe. In both stages of the project, thousands of people at Tate Modern were invited to explore their relationship to production.

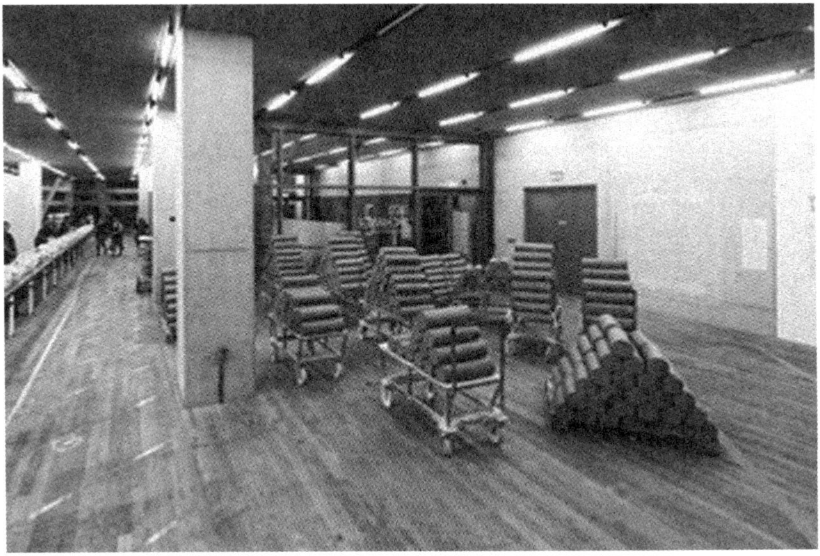

Rolls of Clay
Photograph by Sylvain Deleu

Eight tons of clay were transported from Dudson's factory in Stoke-on-Trent to Tate Modern in to be used in "Factory" as the prime material of production. The clay is produced as rolls to help production in the factory where, at the time, the historic ceramics brand was producing millions of clay objects every year.

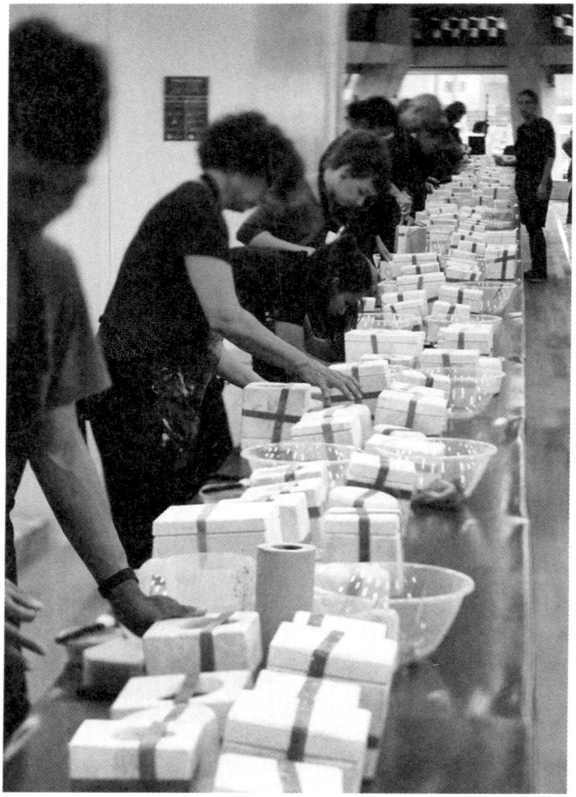

The Production Line
Photograph by Sylvain Deleu

"Factory" was run by factory managers and a workforce of thirty factory workers. The workers were all trained at Tate Modern especially for this project. They learned skills in slip casting and flower making. The public joined them to make over two thousand objects in the weeklong first part of the project.

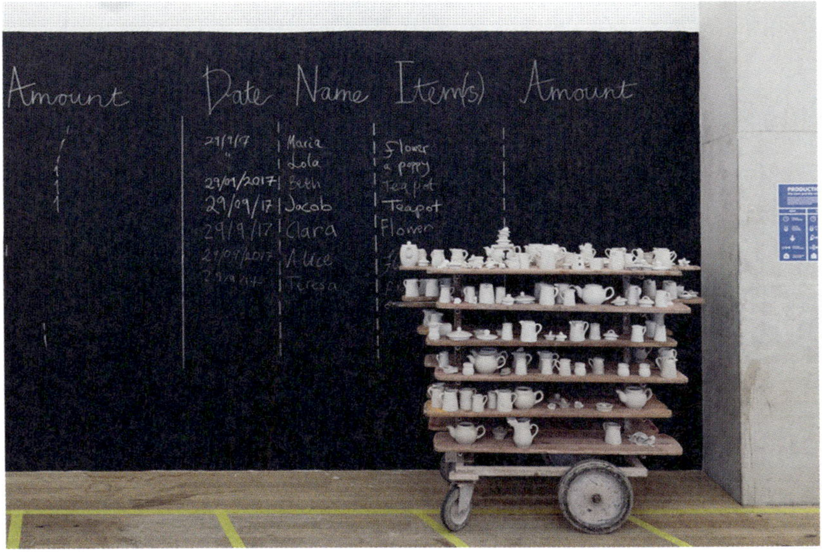

Ware Trolley
Photograph by Matt Greenwood

Rejects from the production line were placed on this trolley. These objects did not get sent to the finished-ware trolleys at the end of the slip-casting line.

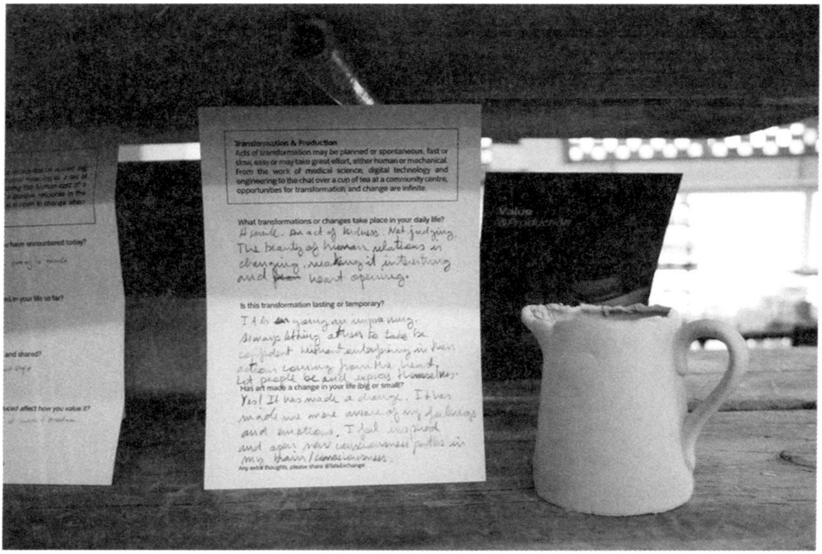

Reflections on Making
Photograph by Sylvain Deleu

These cards were written in the second week, the "redundant" week, when clay production had been suspended and the voices of the public recorded the week before were played back into the redundant "Factory" space. The production line was turned from a place of making into a place of reflection in which the public were asked to add their labor in the form of writing.

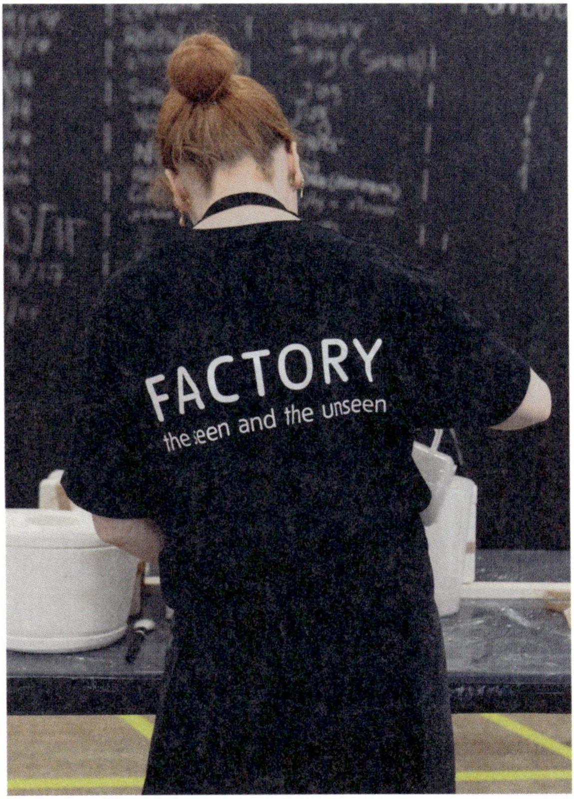

“Factory” Worker
Photograph by Matt Greenwood

One of the workers wearing the project’s uniform, which clearly identified them as distinct from the public and helped them form their “Factory” identity and ownership of the production space.

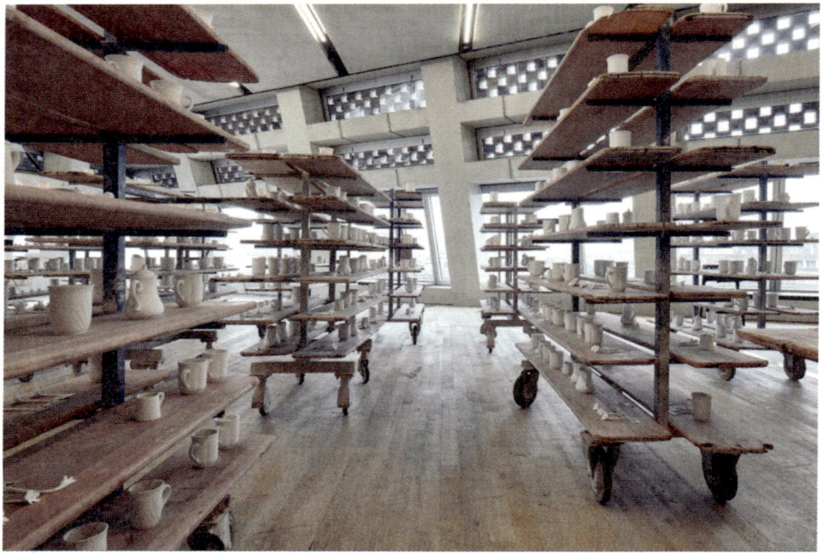

Value in Production
Photograph by Sylvain Deleu

This is the final area in "Factory," where the objects were placed after the production line. At the start of the project, over two thousand objects were already in place on the ware trollies. Throughout the course of the project, the public made more objects and exchanged them with an object made by a previous participant on the trolley, a form of exchange unusual in both industrial and postindustrial production.

THE CRAFTING CRAFTING OF CONCEPTS CONCEPTS CONCEPTS

RICHARD SENNETT & ALEX COLES

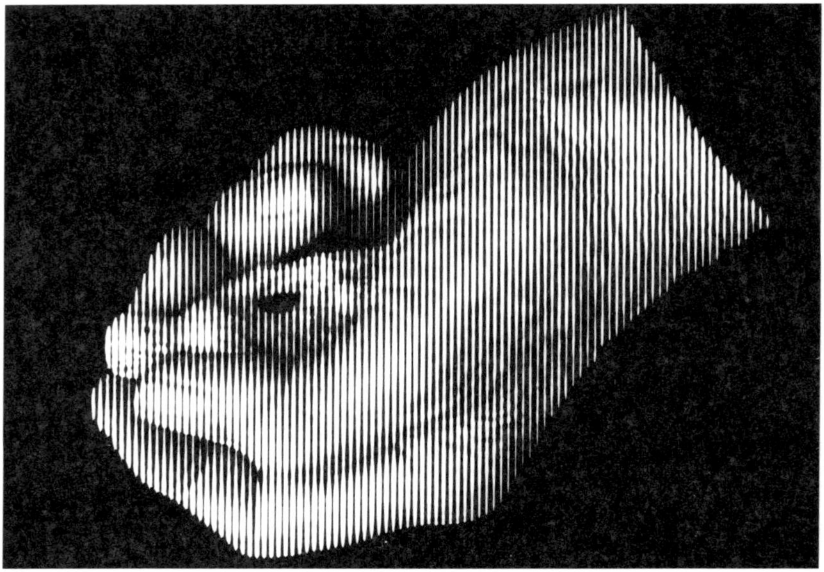

The Crafting of Concepts

Richard Sennett interviewed by Alex Coles

Alex Coles: What led you a decade ago to decide "the craftsman" was an appropriate term for what you wanted to describe?

Richard Sennett: I think it was the right term because in English there is a connection between what craft is and what craftsmanship is, in the sense that the quality of work and the notion that you're doing something very concrete are connected. Seminal to this issue is actual work – work in the abstract doesn't have the same kind of tests of whether it's good or bad. I chose the craftsman because I liked the connection in English between questions of quality and specificity and attachedness and thingness.

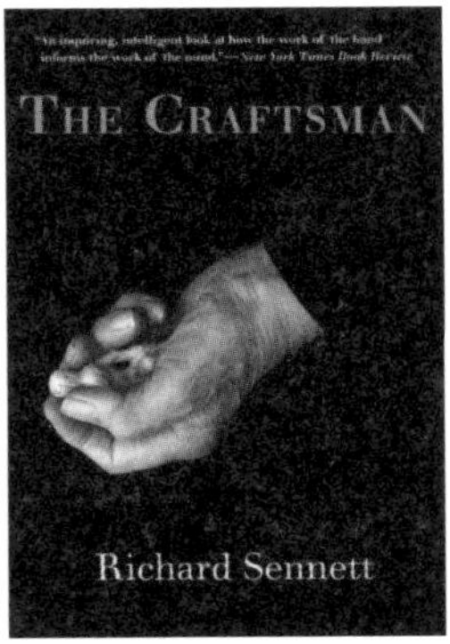

Richard Sennett, *The Craftsman*, Yale University Press, 2008.

AC: Why do you think your book *The Craftsman* (2008) was was so popular at that moment, and what do you think of the way it was so readily taken up by practitioners from across design, architecture, and art?

RS: Think back to that moment: craft was a dead subject. A lot of people knew there was a story there between head and hand – working manually – but it wasn't one that was very present in the discourse at the time. My sense is that craft was taken up because of a discomfort people felt about working predominantly in the digital and losing contact with the tactile. Partly this is to do with the dominance of designing on-screen, but it's also because when doing physical work there are things that you learn about the quality of materials and their resistance to certain types of manipulation that are lost in a purely digital approach to designing. In researching the book, I had numerous discussions with practitioners about their desire to recover a sense of material reality. These discussions revealed the degree to which intellectually and aesthetically artists learn by actually working with physical materials.

But rather than fine art per se, I was drawn to the status of embodiment in creative practices such as choreography, music, and stage design – performing-arts practices that lost touch with the notion of embodiment at the end of the 1980s with the introduction of digital technologies. For example, with music, recordings were exclusively made in the studio, each component of sound being dissected and isolated. The loss of contact with physical presence through live performance concerned me.

But the group of people who became particularly attached to that book were architects. They had been rather islanded by the epoch of theory, whereby a building was seen as a statement rather than a thing to be inhabited. Architects like Shigeru Ban returned a sense of tactility to building by focusing on materials, processes, and textures. A building was a thing to be experienced once again rather than just a theoretical proposal.

AC: Isn't the downside to this revalorization of craft how it has been used by fashion brands to retail luxury products by simply emphasizing the role of the hand or its index?

RS: The commercialization of craft as a luxury good – where the masses get only machine-made goods and those who can afford it handmade ones – is an old story that goes back at least as far as the industrial revolution. There's no solution to it. It's inevitable: capitalism is always trying to capture value. But forms of craft practice do not necessarily need to be part of an elite trade. Think of cooking craft – it's not just those who can afford expensive knives or rarefied ingredients that can practice it. This aspect of craft that plays down consumption is left out too frequently.

AC: Do you think the moment we are currently in has further developed from the one you described a decade ago into one of post-craft?

RS: Of course, it depends on what you mean by craft in the first place. There are new ways of using a computer in a craftsman-like way – you go back and forth between what you draw on-screen and with your hand with greater ease and flexibility. This is identifiable as a craft practice because it's a dialogue with physical practice. If we step out of the framework we've been discussing so far and think about something like, for instance, surgery, where the role of the hand is being expanded, then we see how we are very much still within a craft rather than a post-craft moment.

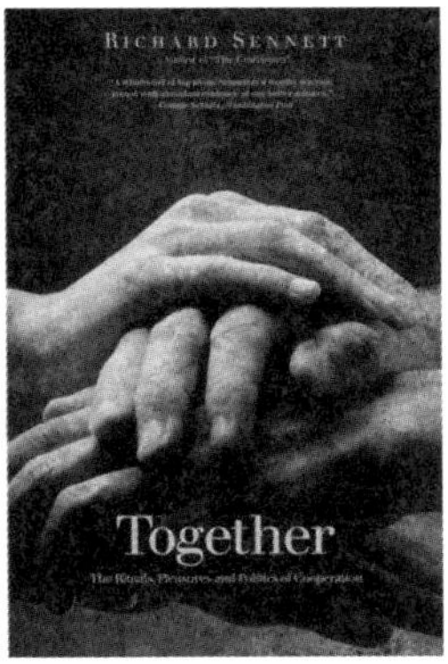

Richard Sennett, *Together: The Rituals, Pleasures and Politics of Cooperation*, Yale University Press, 2012.

AC: Would you revise aspects of *The Craftsman* now in light of the development of your ideas in the past decade, especially those on commonality in your book *Together: The Rituals, Pleasures and Politics of Cooperation* (2012)?

RS: One grows out of the other. I almost called the book on cooperation *The Workshop*. Skills are learned not in isolation from others, but by interacting with them and physical materials. No one learns how to do a thing by following a set of abstract directions: you have to try it out, other people have to criticize you – and this cooperative activity is the classical function of the workshop. To me, the question now is how to develop the equivalent of those classical workshops.

AC: Can you expand on the concept of the classical workshop? How it was initiated and functioned, and the ways you see it being reinvented?

RS: The classical workshop is basically premised on a double relationship, one between the master and the apprentice, and the other between people with different skills and competencies working together. Today that has turned into an unbalanced relationship, with more emphasis on the hierarchical, with the transmitting of knowledge from those who know to those who don't know. There is less emphasis on how people who work together can coordinate with each other through workshop-type structures, and it is this I wanted to focus on.

The workshop is premised on the notion of cooperation, involving working with other people to do things you couldn't do for yourself. It's a natural impulse in human beings, it starts the moment people are born: infants need to work with their parents to be fed, children need to work with their teachers, with their peers, in order to learn, adults obviously need to cooperate to work, to make their communities work, and so on. My concern with this is about complex forms of cooperation: where you are working with people you don't understand, people who are simply different from you, or people you don't like. And to practice those complex forms of cooperation you need skills. That sort of demanding cooperation is a craft.

AC: Could you give a specific example of the kind of cooperation you're talking about?

RS: Take, for instance, an ethnically divided community; the ones I've studied are mostly in the United States, between African Americans and either Koreans or Latinos. Getting along together and making the community work requires suspending the received notion that you'll only cooperate well with people with whom you can identify, whose life experiences are similar to your own. People who are different in those ways need to develop skills – like good listening skills so that they are able to comprehend what people mean. They need empathic skills, know how to express curiosity and to follow up about what somebody else is saying, and to have learned to manage aggression. All of these skills can only be derived from experience.

The final section of *Together* is about coproduction and community dwellers and planners who work together from the start. Coproducing is a way of cooperating but also of craftsmanship. In terms of the latter, it seems to me that the particularity of a given design – its contextual value – is going to be increased by having local people involved from the very beginning. It's a matter of how a design actually interacts with the people who are to inhabit it. The chapter on coproduction in the book attempts to show ways that people who live in a place and the people who are to design it can work together, even if that place is a library or office. Usually what happens in social planning is that the architect shows his designs to the public who are to be consulted, and they are dazzled by an array of renderings whizzed through at a public presentation. At the end of it the planner says, "Does anyone have any questions?" This approach kills off any sense of participation. The kind of planning I'd like to see is much more immersive and dialogue-based.

Being socially competent doesn't mean that when you're faced with challenges you don't fall apart and the social networks of which you are a part don't tear. It involves challenge and risk. Cooperation can also be put to very bad ends: you can be skilled at cooperating and doing harmful things. It's like craftsmanship – it's a technique that can be put to good or bad ends. I'm not very happy with a lot of the discourse around cooperative activity that takes it as a good in itself.

The problem for us today is that learning that kind of social competence so you're able to manage complex situations and work with other people is under threat for various reasons. Modern society is really, ironically, de-skilling people from many of the competences they need to deal with a very complex world, and as a sociologist I'm concerned with the role of institutions in this, especially how they can disable cooperation. The more incompetent people feel themselves to be in dealing with complexity, the more they revert to hostile ways of dealing with the outside world. If you feel competent to manage your own circumstances, you're going to be less defensive and more open. Then there is another model of conversation and debate where you have a conflict between strongly expressed views, and through that creative interaction people come to modify them. Part of the rules of engagement concern having your views vigorously challenged through debate.

In the educational world, we now have extremely rigorous testing regimes for individuals for upward mobility. We don't correspondingly think about organizing educational institutions so the groups of students can study together and talk. Instead, increasingly we use computers to isolate students from communicating with each other so that they learn from each other. The regime places too high a premium on performance instead of exploring ways to use modern communication tools so that people learn together.

AC: Are there other methods that you've developed?

RS: Yes, one I've used extensively in my work is intensive interviewing; once the domain of the ethnographer, today it is at work outside of anthropology and especially in sociology. From this the issue of narrative, which ethnography is all about, assumes a central place. I've also learned a lot from literary theory and from novelists about conducting interviews. This has to do with a particular concern I have, which is how to write in such a way that connects with a reader. And one of the ways to do that is not to hide behind a mask with your readers so that they don't know who's speaking to them. I don't like confessional literature, but I think that if you're trying to speak directly to a reader you need to be able to establish an authorial voice. Otherwise they have no sense of who's talking to them and will disconnect – nothing less than a failure on behalf of the writer in using their own craft.

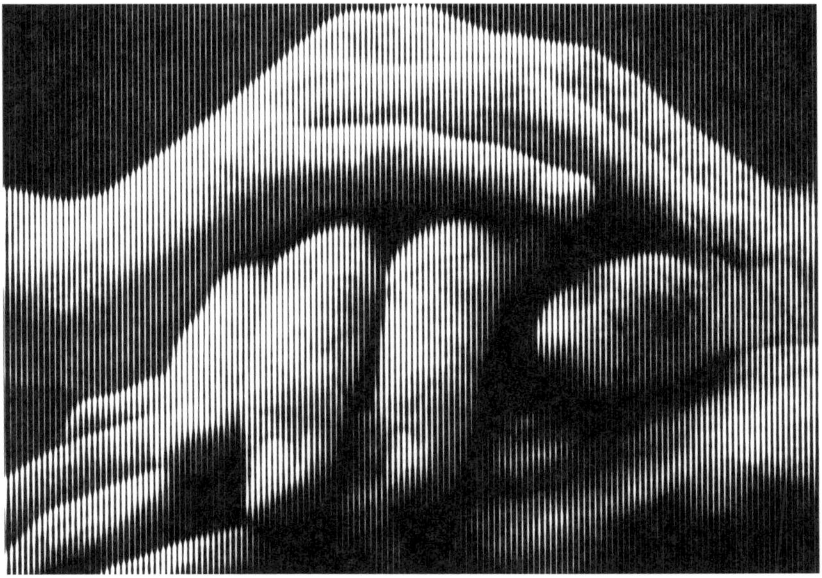

WAR–TORN CRAFT WAR–TORN CRAFT WAR–TORN CRAFT CRAFT CRAFT CRAFT

FLORE DE TAISNE

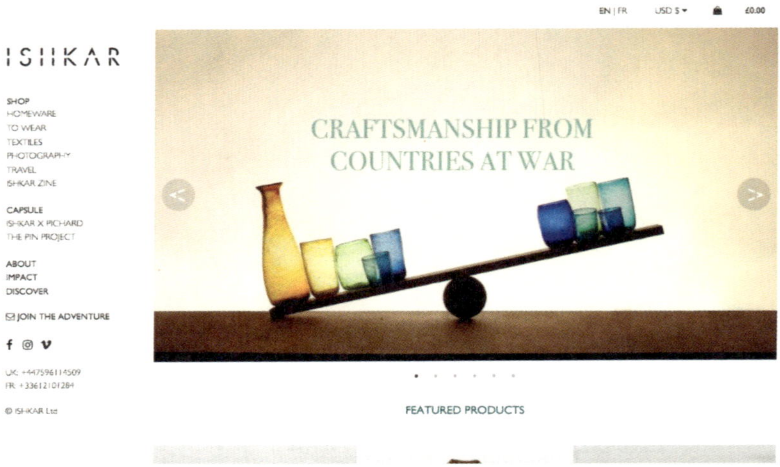

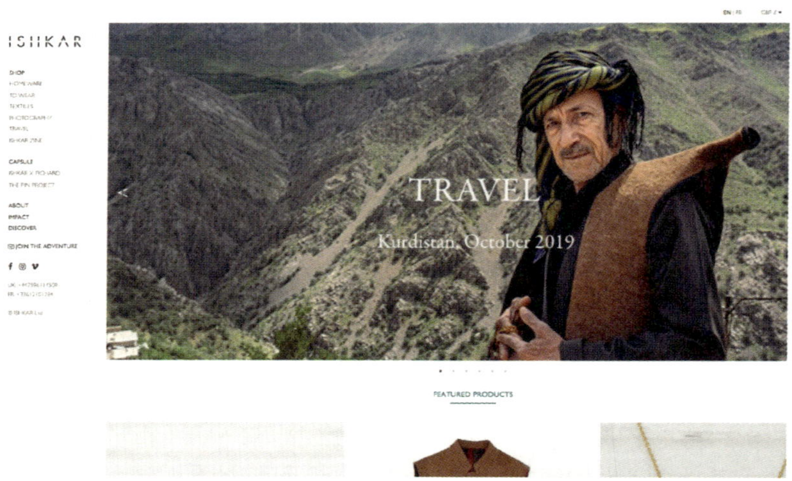

Weaving craft narratives through
Ishkar's website, 2019.

How Ishkar Works

Artisans come up to us saying, “Can you sell this on our behalf?” That’s one way that Iskar works. We also have in-house designers who create pieces alongside artisans. That’s the case for a lot of our collections. Then we have international designers who want to collaborate with us, and it’s a three-way collaboration between the designers, the artisans, and us. This takes a bit longer because we sometimes have to explain to the international designer that they can’t just do this to promote it as a good deed: they have to have this exchange with the artisans. These are the three different ways that we work.

We’re not a charity, so there is a profit margin, but it’s much lower than industry standards. We multiply by two, maximum by three, and that’s not accounting for production costs and our own costs; we have to be sustainable to be able to pay people.

On Crafts Practitioners

Craftspeople are just like designers or artists: there is a flow in what they’re doing that is theirs alone, and to be able to work alongside craftspeople you need to respect that, and you need to work within their time frame. Craftspeople are not makers in the way that they are producing something that has been designed somewhere else or by a designer in the same country; there’s a real dialogue between the maker and the designer, and sometimes the artisan is the designer.

I think in every country most of the difficulties for craftspeople or any small business is exactly the same: selling is difficult, sometimes your kiln doesn’t work, the glazing doesn’t come out the

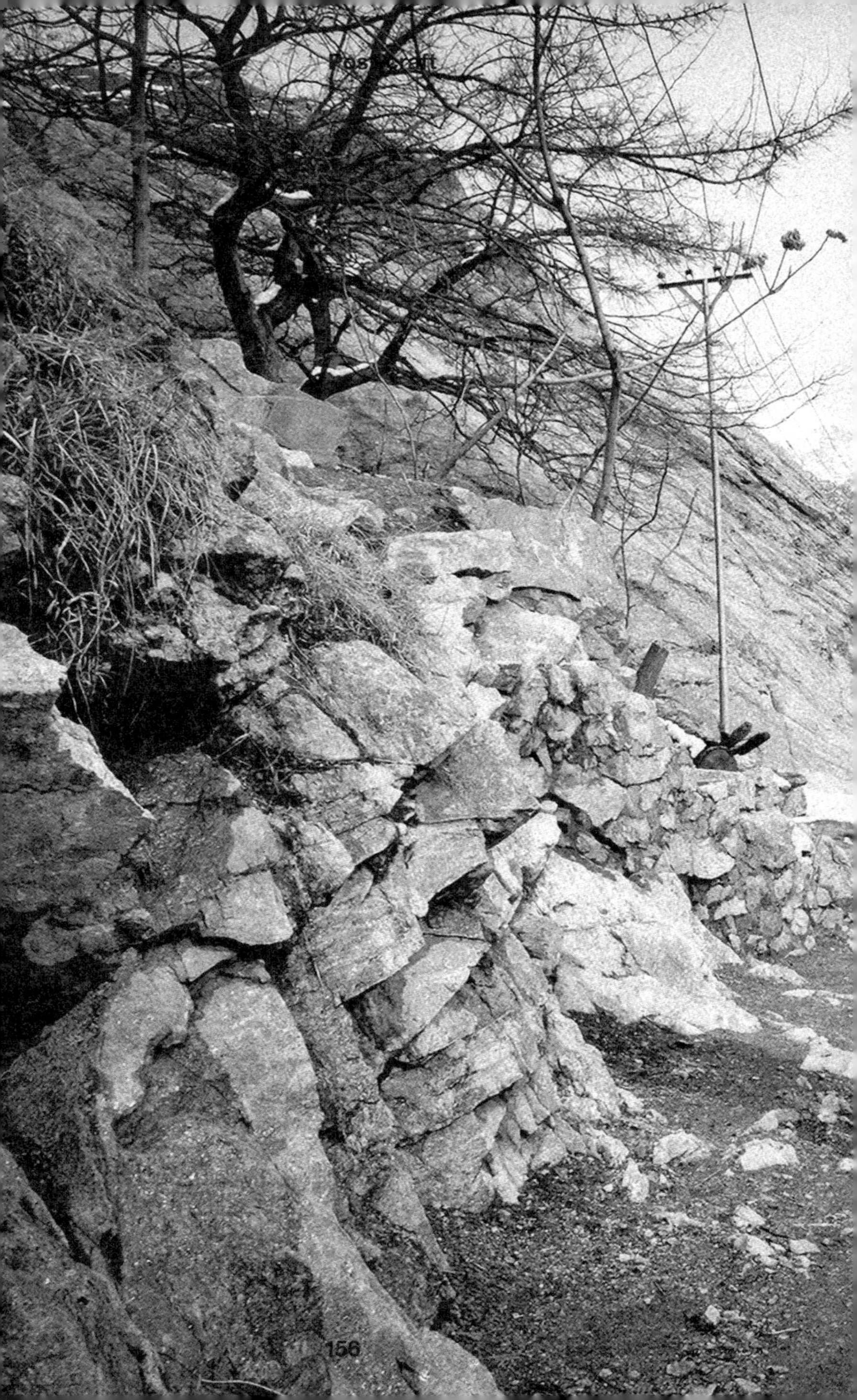

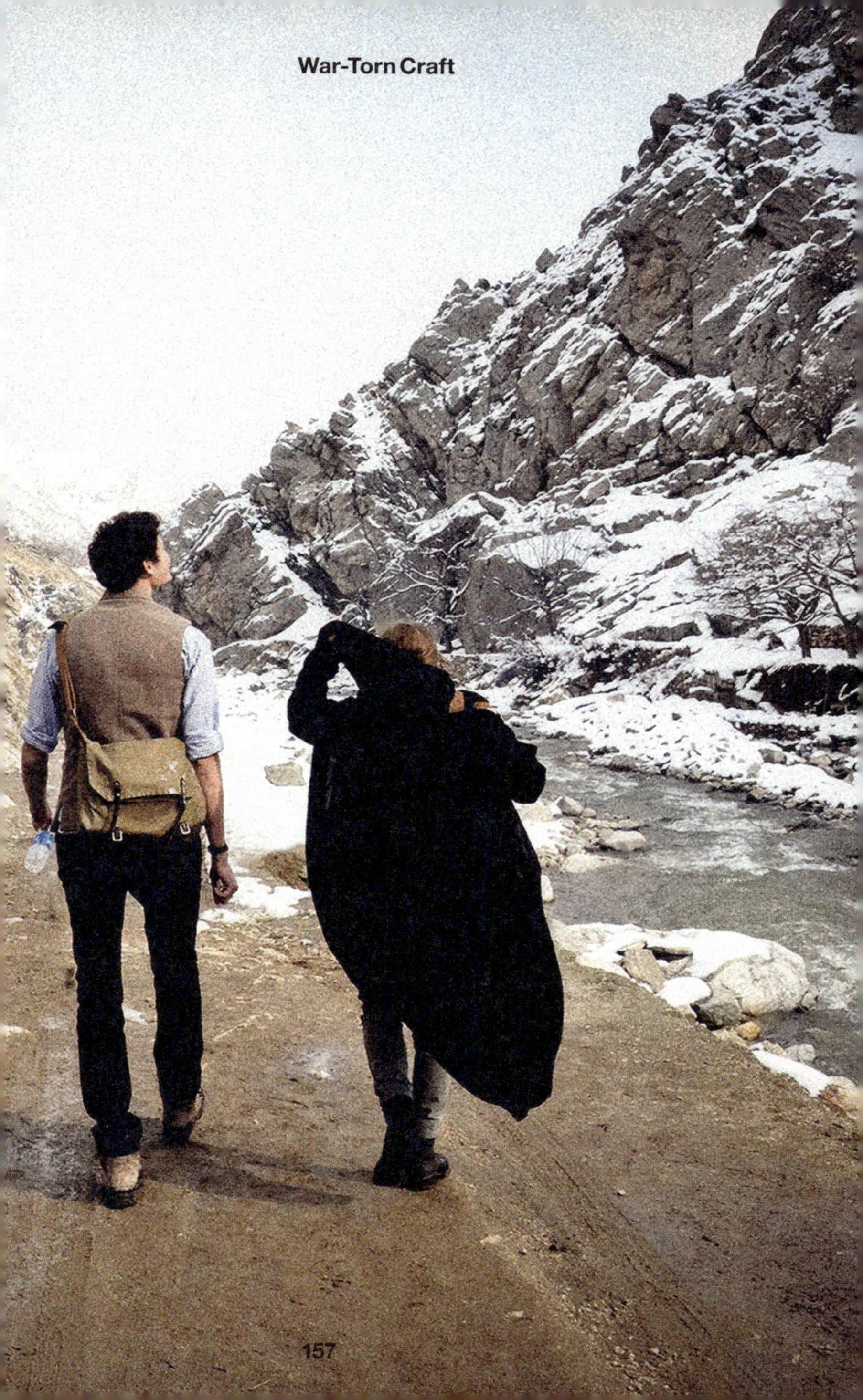

way you wanted so you just throw the objects away, and sometimes it's lonely. And there are additional issues in, say, Yemen or Syria – you sometimes can't go to your workshop because of security issues. But at the core it is not really that, but being a craftsperson, an artisan.

The Local Craft Market

Local demand is very similar to the way it was in France or the United Kingdom thirty years ago. My grandparents stopped buying locally produced, handmade glassware and instead bought pieces made in China probably because the glasses were more practical and could be stacked in the cupboard. For Afghans, Chinese glasses are cheaper and more practical than handblown glasses; the demand is very similar to the demand you can find elsewhere. What is practical, what is cheap.

On Buying Ishkar

Some people buy an object because it's nice and they don't care about where it's made, and some people buy it because they feel a connection – they might be from or have been to the country where it is made, or they could have family members who live in that particular place. Others buy them because artisan producers are generally more appreciated nowadays – they'd rather have a wonky glass than an Ikea glass, which is similar to people buying from the New Craftsmen store in London, for example, or from a glassblower in East London.

I think the fact that people are more conscious of what they are buying, of how they consume things – from what they eat to what they have in their living room – has an impact in terms of what people ask about. We receive a lot of emails

Pages 156–57:

Edmund Le Brun and Flore de Taisne, Ishkar founders, in Afghanistan.

Opposite:

Sankore throw made by Le Ndomo, Segou, Mali, and designed by Rebecca Hoyes, London.

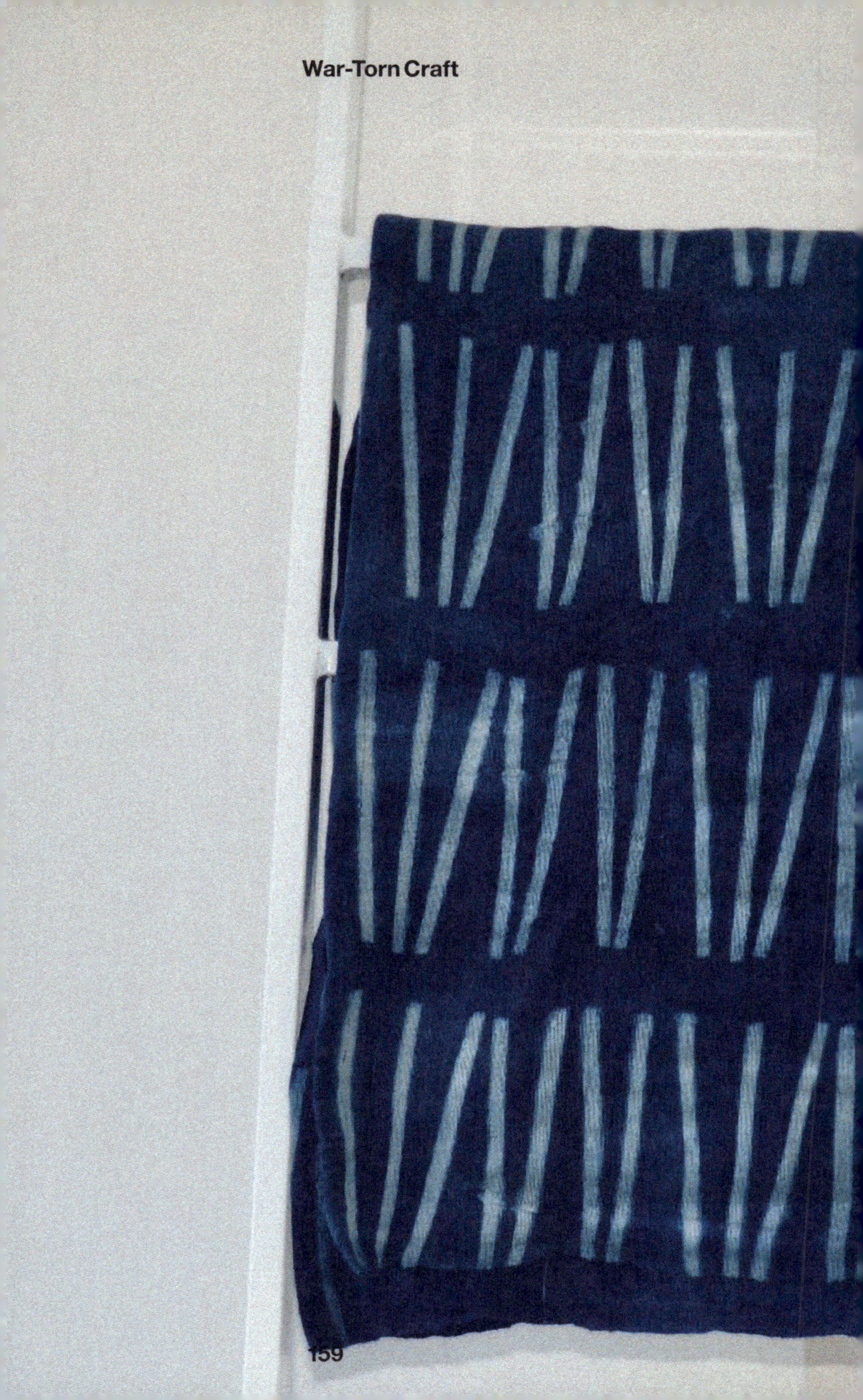

asking where a particular stone is from, or how much we are paying a particular person, or how many days it takes to make a particular tray. People are curious about things that they wouldn't ask another company that makes the same products industrially.

It shouldn't just be wealthy people who are empowered or able to buy "ethical products." We feel that everyone should be able to buy a stack ring for thirty-eight pounds and understand the story and ethics behind it.

On the Problem of "Craft"

If the word craft is associated with non-Western countries such as Afghanistan, some people think that it refers to those trinkets that you find at a charity stall, that you buy for five pounds and feel good about, those sort of crafty pieces. The word craft was quite charged beforehand, and now it is less so, but it is used slightly too much, as with "handcrafted chips."

We use the word artisan much more; *artisanale* – or *artisanat d'art*, which has different connotations – is the French word for craft. Artisan is more linked to art and to time, rather than to slightly poor-quality trinkets you might buy to accessorize your table. You have all these different words that have slightly different meanings. So we still use the terms craftsmen and crafted, but we wouldn't really describe the objects as being craft pieces – we would just describe them as products or artisanal. I think that the semantics is really interesting. But at least for us it is slightly different because of this additional West/East layer: this dynamic use of the word craft in many places. There are other words that Ishkar needs to work on, and the craft element is the least of our worries.

Opposite:

Afghan glassblower Ghulam Sekhi in his mud-brick workshop in Herat.

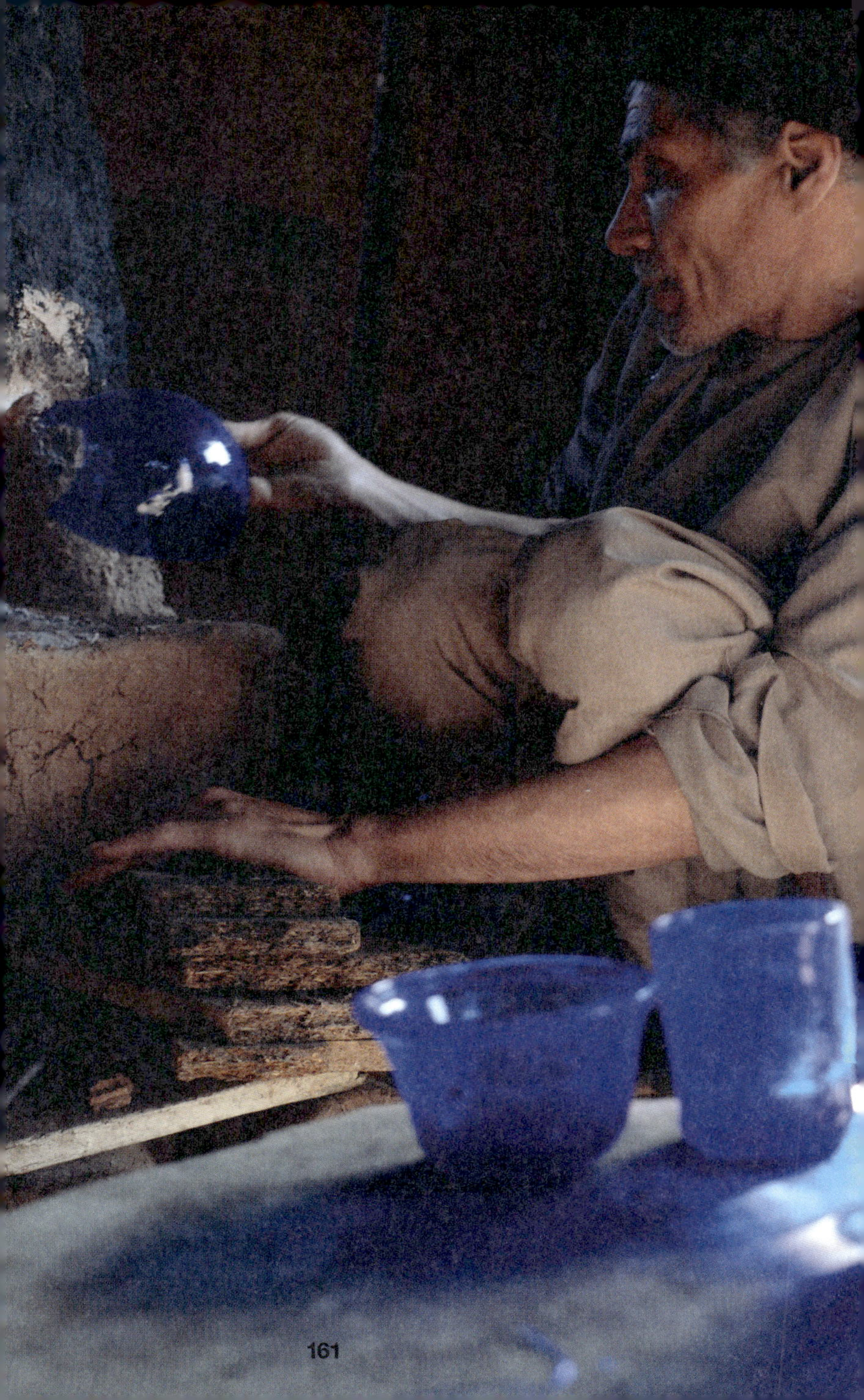

Storytelling

We talk about the craftspeople we work with the same way as you would about British designer Sebastian Cox. We wouldn't use the word poor; we rarely use the word refugee. We ask the crafts practitioners to write their own bios, and we work a lot on communicating who we are doing this for. If promoting a British jeweler, for example, would you want people to know that she's struggling with raising her three kids as a single mother? Maybe yes, maybe no, but it's for her to say, to put forward.

It's making sure that whatever narrative they want to give is the one we share.

If we are posting something on Instagram, we think about what a particular picture conveys. Is it conveying pity? Is it conveying pride? Is it conveying hard work? Is it conveying nostalgia? Is it conveying the meaning associated with that particular image or story?

On Criticism of Ishkar

Through our Instagram account, we have received backlash against how we work. One of the many things people have questioned is why we only work with white designers. I think the conversation is an ongoing one, and we try to be as transparent as possible about the way we do things. We might start being slightly more open, saying, for example, that an Afghan designer or maker reached out to us.

We haven't felt we wanted to do that because Ishkar is just a platform for showcasing what artisans are doing, and we thought the logic behind it would be understood – that we're not pitying them or putting them in a specific box.

So I think the dynamic of designer and maker – and I'm speaking as a French person – and the difficulty of the designer and the maker dynamic exists, even in the city, between a Parisian designer and a Parisian maker. But the dynamic is exacerbated or can be under a lot of scrutiny, if the designers are from the United Kingdom and are working with makers from somewhere else, for example, India or Thailand.

Yes, Edmund and I are white, and yes, we are doing what we're doing, but we try as much as possible to visit the places we talk about. We even did a photography project with local photographers. For us to be sort of their agents and sell their work is a way for us to try as much as possible to let people talk about what they want talk about. We've been receiving criticism that we make money from poor people, that we cripple the individual – we never said that anywhere, we never describe ourselves like that. We share with the artisans our website, we ask them to review lots of different things, we tag them on our Instagram posts.

Holidaying with Ishkar

In 2019, Ishkar started offering trips, opening up its craft countries to intrepid travelers. Starting with Iraqi Kurdistan and Bamiyan in Afghanisation, the company promises opportunities to experience a different side of these countries from the war-torn one seen in the headlines.

The whole experience thing is key to how people relate to a brand – and so that's what we thought, if you want to go beyond set of glasses or jewelry pieces you can just come with us.

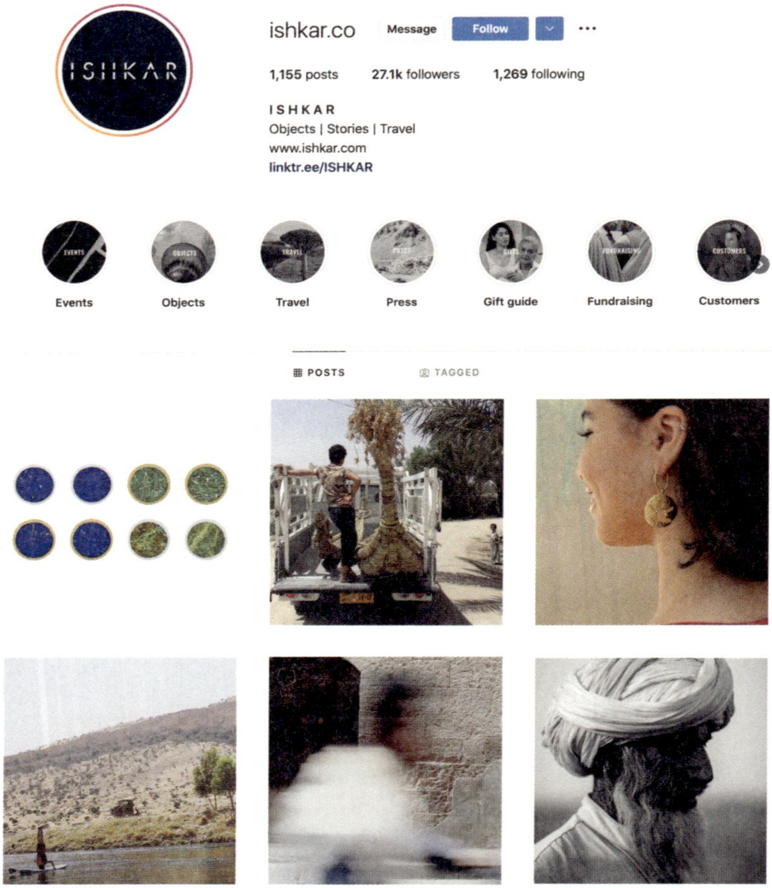

Ishkar's Instagram account.

Opposite:

Profiling Afghan jeweller Saeeda Etebari on Ishkar's Instagram feed, 2019.

Announcing the launch of Pietra Dura coasters made by Pakistani artisan Zargey, 2019.

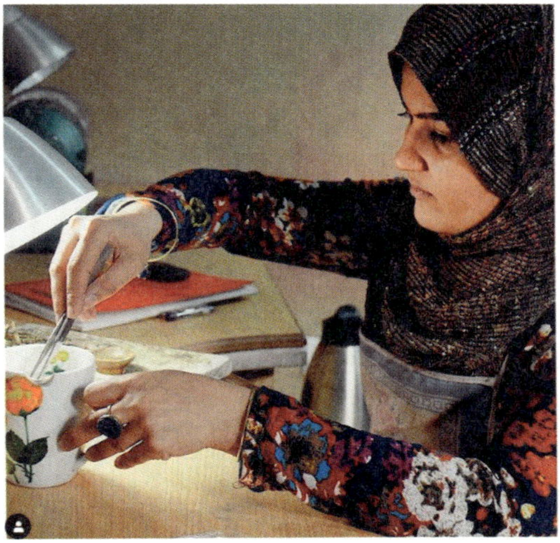

ishkarartisans • Follow ···

ishkarartisans Meet Saeeda Etebari, one of the most impressive designers and jewellers we work with. Last year Saeeda designed a collection of striking and contemprary pieces for ISHKAR, inspired by the energy of Kabul, the city where she makes them. Available online now, link in bio.

29w

ishkarartisans #artisan #jewellery #jeweller #handmade #designerjewellery #madeinafghanistan #craft #heritage #whomadeyourjewelry #fashionrevolution #ethicalfashion #emerald #silver #brass #jewellerydesign

173 likes

JANUARY 7

Log in to like or comment.

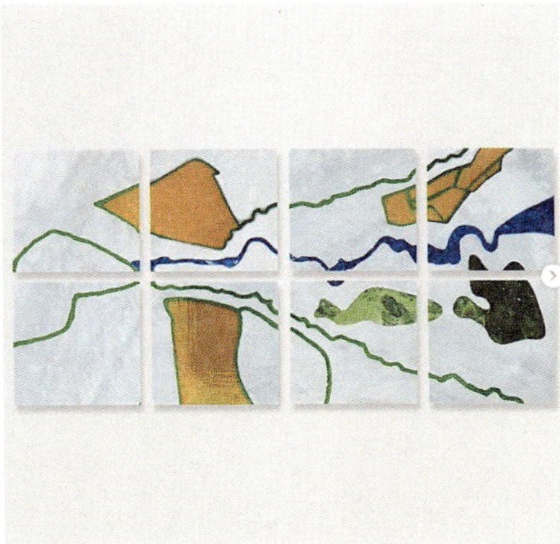

ishkarartisans • Follow ···

ishkarartisans We have just launched our latest collection: handcrafted, pieta dura coasters, now available to purchase exclusively on our website (link in bio). Made by Zargey, a master artisan @thelelcollection in Pakistan. For the last two decades the LÉL Collection has worked tirelessly with Afghan refugees in Peshawar to preserve, reinterpret and evolve the ancient art of pietra dura.
The landscape inspired pattern for each of our coasters is chiselled out of a marble base by hand, before being fitted with precisely hand cut slices of lapis lazuli, serpentine, ammozonite and resin.

125 likes

NOVEMBER 4, 2018

Log in to like or comment.

Reading Ishkar

In 2019, Ishkar launched ISHKAR_ZINE: A Journal on Conflict, Culture and Craftsmanship. *Filled with reflections on the state of the craft industry and the craft revival as well as stories on local history and crafts, such as Afghan war rugs and the ancient Arab interest in Greek philosophy, the print magazine aims to provide a different perspective on countries reported on more often for their wars than their rich cultures and traditions.*

Opposite:

ISHKAR_ZINE: A Journal on Conflict, Culture and Craftsmanship, 2019.

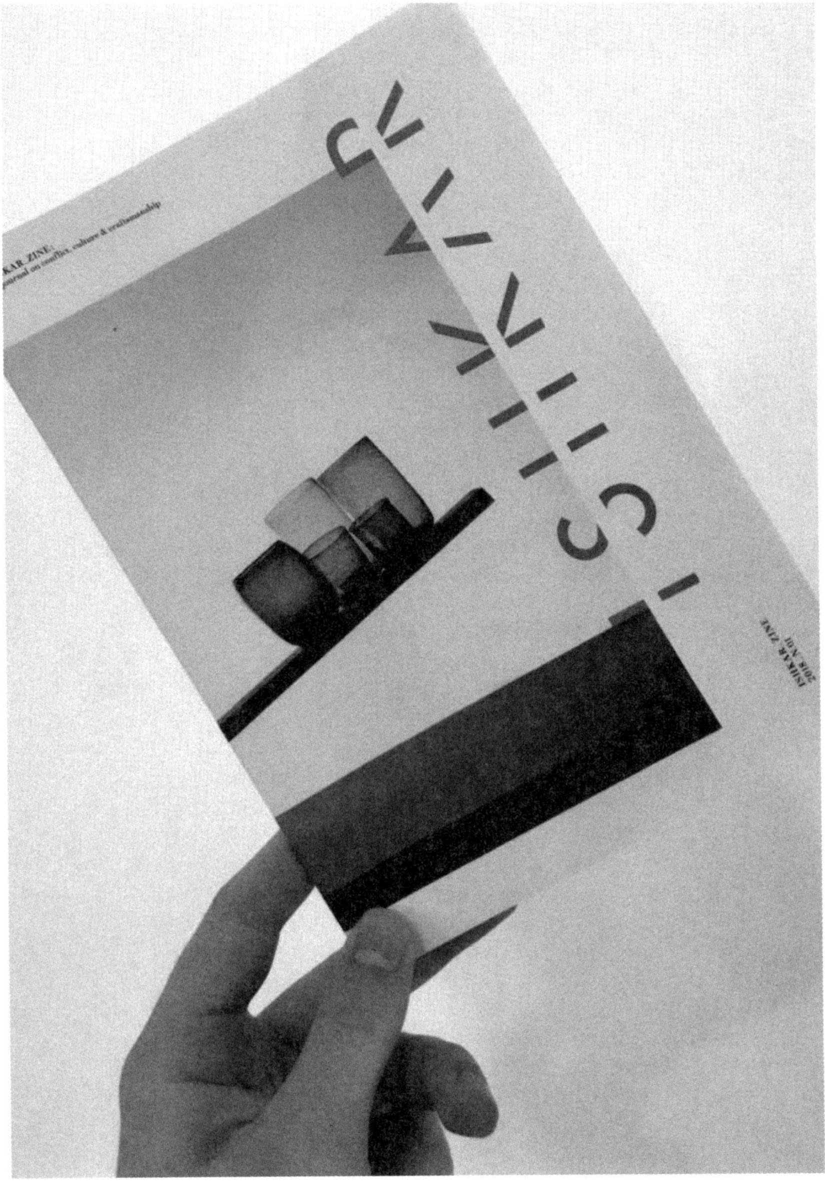

Acknowledgments

A lot of life happened during the making of this book, which originated as a symposium at the Institute of Contemporary Arts in London in 2015. And a lot has happened in the world since the texts were put together between 2016 and 2018 and edited in 2021. Special thanks goes to our patient authors; the ICA team and symposium speakers Revital Cohen & Tuur Van Balen, Rosario Hurtado and Roberto Feo, Sam Jacob, Dr. Stephen Knott, and Dr. Jana Scholze; Lydia Catterall, Stan Portus, Jane Smith, Sophie McKinlay, Verina Gfader, Toby Webster, Caroline Schneider, Niamh Dunphy, Max Bach, the Kingston School of Art at Kingston University London, and the School of Arts and Humanities at the University of Huddersfield.

Colophon

Front cover:

Basra in my sights by Andy, HMP Everthorpe (detail), from "You Have the Watches, We Have the Time," 2013, organized by Jeremy Deller for the British Pavilion, 55th Venice Biennale. Photo by Cristiano Corte.

EP / Volume 3
Post-craft

Published by Sternberg Press

Editor in chief: Alex Coles
Volume editors: Alex Coles, Catharine Rossi
Managing editors: Max Bach, Niamh Dunphy
Image research: Lydia Catterall
Graphic design: Experimental Jetset
Printing: KOPA, Kaunas, Lithuania

ISBN 978-3-95679-395-0

Distributed by The MIT Press, Art Data,
Les presses du réel, and Idea Books

Previous volumes in the EP series:

Design Fiction
Edited by Alex Coles, with EP In-Lab

The Italian Avant-Garde, 1968–1976
Edited by Alex Coles and Catharine Rossi

Sternberg Press
71–75 Shelton Street
London WC2H 9JQ
www.sternberg-press.com